Henry Edward Manning

The Temporal Power of the Vicar of Jesus Christ

Henry Edward Manning

The Temporal Power of the Vicar of Jesus Christ

ISBN/EAN: 9783744652575

Printed in Europe, USA, Canada, Australia, Japan

Cover: Foto ©Lupo / pixelio.de

More available books at **www.hansebooks.com**

THE
TEMPORAL POWER
OF THE
VICAR OF JESUS CHRIST.

Ballantyne Press
BALLANTYNE, HANSON AND CO.
EDINBURGH AND LONDON

THE TEMPORAL POWER

OF THE

VICAR OF JESUS CHRIST.

BY

HENRY EDWARD,
CARDINAL ARCHBISHOP OF WESTMINSTER.

Third Edition, with a Preface.

LONDON: BURNS AND OATES.
1880.

CONTENTS.

	PAGE
PREFACE TO THE THIRD EDITION . . .	ix
GENERAL PREFACE	xvii

PART FIRST.
The Origin of the Temporal Power.

LECTURE I.

The Temporal Power first shown in the Ancient Patrimonies of the Church 1

LECTURE II.

The Temporal Power again appears in the Formation and Preservation of Christian Society 30

LECTURE III.

The Dissolution of Christian Society the necessary consequence of the Overthrow of the Temporal Power . 54

PART SECOND.
The Perpetual Conflict of the Vicar of Jesus Christ.

LECTURE I.

The Mystery of Iniquity, which had already begun to work in the days of the Apostles, the principle of this conflict; its consequences, the denial of the Incarnation and of Authority 81

LECTURE II.

The Person of Antichrist the last Head of the Mystery of Iniquity 103

LECTURE III.

The Vicar of Jesus Christ in his twofold sovereignty the Supernatural Antagonist of the Mystery of Iniquity and of Antichrist 117

LECTURE IV.

The Persecution of the Head of Iniquity against the Vicar of Jesus Christ, and the Destruction of the Mystery of Evil and its Head 142

PART THIRD.

The last Glories of the Holy See greater than the first.

LECTURE I.

The Glory of the Supernatural Life and Constancy of the Holy See always more clearly proved in the Height of Persecutions 177

LECTURE II.

The Present Time, which seems darkest by Persecutions, will appear in the result brightest in Glory . . . 196

LECTURE III.

The Future Glories of the Pontificate of Pius IX. . . 218

PREFACE TO THE THIRD EDITION.

THE following pages were first published in separate parts about 1860. They were collected and republished in a second edition in 1861.

1. When they were written, Pius IX. held Rome and the States of the Church in their integrity; but he was already hemmed in by revolutions and conspiracies. France and Italy had invaded Lombardy. Tuscany, Parma, and Modena, and a little later the kingdom of Naples, were in the hands of the Revolution. It was evident that, by fraud or by force, or, as it ended, by both, Rome would be entered and usurped. Nevertheless, the hopes of some were stronger than their foresight; and we were told that it would never be. But others thought that what had happened already nine times might happen once more.

2. The history of the ten years between 1860 and 1870 is marked by a series of political and diplomatic frauds unequalled in history. The seizure of Ancona and the Marches, of Bologna and the

Romagnas; the Convention of 1864 between France and Italy, by which Italy bound itself to respect, and even to protect, the Holy See; the Garibaldian conspiracies and invasions; the duplicity of Sardinia; the complicity and countenance of Napoleon III., are all too well known to need more than recital.

3. The French Empire was then in its pride of place in Europe. Austria had failed before it. Italy was its ward, and Rome was under its protection. The military power of France was believed to be the greatest in the world; but there were those who foretold its downfall. It had presided over the undermining of the temporal sovereignty of the Vicar of Jesus Christ. While apparently protecting Rome, Italy was permitted by French statesmen, and even countenanced, in a policy which had publicly claimed Rome for capital.

4. On the 20th of September 1870, the Italian armies bombarded and entered Rome, but on the 4th of the same month the French Empire had already ceased to be, and Napoleon III. was a prisoner in Germany. Twice in this century France has had to learn this lesson: No man who lays hand on the Vicar of Christ has ever prospered; has ever escaped the rod.

5. What is sketched out in the two earlier parts of

these pages is already fulfilling. The usurpation of Rome has sent disturbance throughout the continent of Europe. Italy first, and above all, feels the recoil of its violence. Every political question is complicated with a religious contention. Its unity as a nation is hindered by its divisions in religion and conscience. It was forced into Rome by a revolution, and the Revolution holds the gates so that it cannot withdraw. The old and solid monarchy of Savoy is trembling to its fall in Rome. The Revolution which brought it there is its master.* Germany committed the same folly. In the hour of its political unity it divided itself by a religious conflict with the Catholic Church. It was beguiled and driven into the Falk Laws, which, after persecuting the weak, can only bring defeat and shame to the German Empire. In Switzerland, the so-called Liberal party of infidels and "Old Catholics" has persecuted and spoiled the Church. In France, the Republic has been growing every year more anti-Catholic, and now the Ferry Laws have brought it into direct collision with the Church. The period of indifference is already passing into the period of coercive or penal legislation. Liberals are now persecutors, and republican freedom refuses liberty to

* See "The Independence of the Holy See," chap. iv. Kegan Paul, London.

conscience. Whether this will pass away, no man knoweth. All things point to another and a violent issue. It is more likely that a collision between the revolutionary policy of the Continent and the Catholic Church will follow after these preludes of unjust repression and petty persecution. In Italy, Germany, Switzerland, and France, the Governments have entered upon the period of conflict.

6. And this disturbance will last and become more intense so long as the Head of the Christianity of the world is violently thrust from his place among the nations and powers of Christendom. Rome was never yet usurped but the whole of Europe was shaken; and peace has never been restored in Europe but Rome has returned again to the Vicar of Jesus Christ. At this moment every country in Europe is threatened by revolution; and the revolutions of Europe, from the Communism of France to the Nihilism of Russia, are becoming one and universal. Their confluence will probably be in the Socialism of Germany. Against these dangers at home, and against armed invasions from abroad, all the powers of Europe are under arms. Eleven millions of armed men are draining every country of its industry and of its youth. A voluntary disarmament is as hopeless as the return of the reign of Astraea upon earth. They will never lay down

their arms till they have disarmed each other on the fields of battle. They have heaped up judgment against themselves, and they will be left to execute it. Every man's sword shall be against his brother. As the moral power which governed Europe becomes less, the material force becomes greater. Faith and love and right are pushed aside, and an age of iron reigns in their stead. I laid no claim to be a prophet in forecasting what has come to pass; but I little thought twenty years ago to live to see so many of these foresights already fulfilled.

7. There is one point in which the present crisis of the Holy See and of the Christian world differs from all that has gone before it. Always in the ages past, when one or more of the European powers were in conflict with the Holy See, one or more of the other powers were friendly and gave it protection. Now not one stands in its defence. They have all, with one accord, hid their faces from the Vicar of our Lord. Some have violently wronged him; others have connived, through fear or complicity, and all are like Saul, who kept the clothes of those who stoned Stephen. They are all consenting in the deed: some by expressed assent, others by silence when they ought to speak. Of the hireling St. Gregory the Great says, "Fugisti quia tacuisti." The princes and rulers of Christendom

have forsaken their master, and their silence in the hour of danger is flight.

Never till now have all the nations of Europe consented in the deed of those who have usurped Rome. Never till now has the public law of Europe been changed to sanction the usurpation. For the first time the Head of Christendom is excluded from the Senate of Christian sovereigns.

This universal abandonment, and common acquiescence in the wrongs of the Vicar of Jesus Christ, is the characteristic of the present crisis. And as it is the climax of the wrong, so it will be the decisive point in the conflict, and in the restitution of Christian Europe, if indeed its Christian order shall ever be restored. Of this I know nothing. It may be that as the dispensation of grace to the nations of the East ran out when Mahometanism came in like a flood over the four schismatical Patriarchates and four hundred Christian Sees, so it may be the times of grace may be running out to the nations of the West for their rebellion against the Church and the Vicar of our Lord. But these things are not for us to reason about.

8. In reading over these pages, I have been conscious that at times I have used words of strong condemnation; and a tone sharper than I believe I have usually adopted. But when it is borne in

mind that at the time I wrote only ten years had passed since the tempest about Papal Aggression; that a new penal law had been enacted against the Bishops of the Catholic Church; that the language of controversy was fierce and contemptuous on all sides of me; that hardly a week passed without some denunciations of the Pontifical Government in the press or in Parliament; that the influence of England, by its diplomacy and by its statesmen, was driving and cheering onward the Sardinian, Mazzinian, Garibaldian revolution against Rome; that any one who stood and spoke for the temporal power, or even for the spiritual authority of the Pope, was assailed and derided by name—a fate which, to my consolation then and now, largely befell me; when all these things are calmly and fairly weighed, I think I shall not be censured as having exceeded the measure of *inculpata tutela*, or of legitimate self-defence which the law of nature gives to every man in behalf of himself and of his duty. There is not, I believe, from first to last, to be found a word that is personal to any man, nor an assault against anything that lies out of the reach of fair public conflict.

9. Lastly, I cannot fail to note the change which has passed over England in these last twenty years. Then its attitude towards the Catholic Church

abroad and at home was sensibly hostile, and the utterances of its public opinion were unjust. Now it has returned to itself. It is not the nature of Englishmen to be little, bitter, or unfair. The public feeling of England towards the Catholic Church, by twenty years of experience and better knowledge, is now fair and kindly. I do not say that the people of England are nearer to the Catholic faith; but I am sure that they have learned to know more truly what we believe, and are half amused and half ashamed at themselves for believing in the scares and the superstitions of their fathers as to the idolatries of our faith and the conspiracies of our practice.

If I had to speak again on these things now, I could say much which then would not have been true. If I had spoken then as it would be possible to speak now, I should have failed in fidelity, for plain-speaking is fidelity to truth.

HENRY EDWARD,
Cardinal Archbishop of Westminster.

WESTMINSTER,
March 14, 1880.

GENERAL PREFACE.

In reprinting the three small Treatises which form the present volume, it may be well to prefix a few words to excuse their insufficiency as compared with the great subject of the Temporal Power,—of which no one is more aware than I am. I am not ashamed of saying, that when this, which has become the leading and critical question of these times, not only for Catholics, but for the nations of Europe, first was forced upon us, I was but little prepared to conceive its vast extent and its vital importance. I had been used to regard it as a sacred institution of Divine Providence, related chiefly to the beautiful confederation of Europe in the ages of Faith, surviving into present times as an object of veneration rather than as a vital power of government. It seemed rather to be a monument of the majesty, beauty, and splendour of the past, than an instrument of energy in the present, fitted for the vehement action of our modern world, and mingling with all the conflicts of the nineteenth century. Neither am I ashamed to confess that I did not apprehend the reasons of the Divine conduct in its institution, nor its titles of just and sovereign right, nor its relation to the future action of the Church upon the world, as I have learned to perceive them now. They grew upon me as I read, and have manifested themselves with such a light of evidence and such a continually increasing importance, that I had hardly finished any part of the following pages without at once feeling dissatisfied. And when I had reached the end, I wished that I might have begun all over again. I believe, however, that in the following pages the full outline of the subject is described, and that no error in principle will be found. But that everything ought to be treated with a far greater fulness of illustration, expansion, and detail, I am altogether aware. Nevertheless, such as they are, I am compelled to let them stand, forasmuch as I see no hope of finding the leisure necessary to begin them afresh. All that I can now do, is to prefix a few words in which I may in some degree supply what is wanting.

I have therefore reviewed, in a summary way, the periods of the formation of the Temporal Power, tracing out its attitude under Paganism, and under the Byzantine Emperors and the abandonment of Italy, from which dates its proper manifestation. It was then finally liberated from all civil subjection, and left to be the sole occupant of Rome; until it was clothed by the necessity of events with a supreme administration, and finally by the voice of the people with a proper sovereignty. Now although this is but a tracing in outline, it indicates the points and the connection of the evidence. But, in treating of this subject in the present day, it is necessary to bear in mind the condition of the social and political system of Europe, and to meet the modern theories of revolution and of popular rights. To do so, as it ought to be done, single paragraphs in the following lectures would become treatises, and single lectures volumes. Nevertheless, I have endeavoured to bear these points in mind, touching them as I could by the way, and not losing sight of them even when not explicitly stated.

Inasmuch as they were addressed to Englishmen, it was necessary that certain matters and modes of speech should be admitted which would be hardly intelligible in Catholic or in other countries. There is perhaps no people in the world among whom it is more difficult to speak of the Temporal Power of the Pope than among Englishmen. The first axioms of the Christian ecclesiastical polity, which in Catholic countries all men believe, in England have been simply effaced by the Reformation. The state of political opinion in England is even more opposed to it than that of the United States: for among us there is not only less indifference, but there is a traditional animosity against the Holy See, especially in its relations to Temporal Power, which Englishmen draw with their first breath, and cherish by all their education, literature, and prejudice.

But besides these special features of the political condition of this country, there is also a general law in the history of Christian and Catholic truth which must be taken into the account.

There is a certain progression in the manifestation of error. The Gnosticism of the East pervaded the early ages, and threw out a whole line of heresies in opposition to the mysteries of the Holy Trinity and of the Incarnation. The Councils of Nice and of Florence may be taken as the two wings of the Church's array against the heresies of the East. The materialism of the West has occupied the later ages with a line of heresies, all of which more or less deny the supernatural order. Pelagianism and Protestantism may be taken as the two extremes, and the Councils of Orange and of Trent as the right and the left of the Catholic Theology, by which the Church has defined and manifested the presence and action of the supernatural order.

Now this seems to me to give a fair indication of the kind of errors with which we have to deal in England. They are by no means Oriental, that is, speculative, subtil, metaphysical, or abstract; but emphatically Western, that is, material, sensuous, rationalistic, and secular. Protestantism is a revolt against the supernatural, against sacramental grace, against the jurisdiction of the Church over souls, against the transmission of its Divine office, against the power of binding and loosing, against the abiding Presence of Jesus in the Holy Sacrament and Sacrifice of the Altar, against the supernatural unity and endowments of the Mystical Body, against the office of the Vicar of the Incarnate Word in the spiritual and temporal prerogatives conferred upon his person.

Now all these are kindred errors, the offspring of one stem. They are no more than so many detailed denials of the supernatural order, and of the presence and operation of the powers of the Incarnation upon man and upon society. Pelagius denied the presence of interior supernatural grace in our regeneration; Luther in our justification; modern Protestantism in the Church; and in Christendom which is its creation and its product.

To a Catholic the Holy Sacraments and the Church are consequences of the Incarnation,—virtues and creative powers which go forth from the Person of our Incarnate Lord. We cannot contemplate them except in union with Him and by the light of Divine Faith. They are facts and phenomena of the supernatural order. We cannot treat them by any natural calculus, or test them by chemistry or by physical analysis. Though they be in contact with the natural order, there is in them a supernatural element which transcends all natural tests. In their contact with the natural order they may be contemplated in part by the instruments of evidence and the criteria of historical truth. But such tests are partial, and such appreciations are inadequate. For instance, be it reverently said, the Presence of our Incarnate Lord on earth was an object of sense to the Jews, who called Him the Son of the Carpenter; and of reason to Nicodemus, who inferred from His works that He was a Teacher sent from God; but of faith to St. Peter, to whom a light was given to see the presence of One of whom flesh and blood can make no revelation.

In like manner, in the perpetuity of this same Divine Presence in the Holy Eucharist sense may contemplate the species, and reason define the fact of this supernatural change of substance; but the manner of the Divine action transcends the natural order, and can be contemplated alone, as the holy Council of Trent teaches,* "though we can scarcely express it in words, by the understanding illuminated by faith."

So also in the Church, which—with its four notes of unity, sanctity, universality, and apostolicity; its three properties of unity, visibility, and perpetuity; and its three endowments of indefectibility, infallibility, and authority—constitutes an object of sense in its visible presence, of reason in its history and action on the nations of the world, and of faith in its supernatural powers and divine commission on earth.

And if this be so of the whole Body of the Church, it is so eminently and emphatically of its Visible Head; for the endowments of the Body are the prerogatives of the Head, and what is to be found pervading the body and its members, is to be found, by way of eminence and of excellence, and as it were typically, in the Head; for the Head not only bears a proportion of eminence and excellence to the whole Body, but also a relation of proportion and representation to the unseen Head, in whom all fulness dwells.

---

* "Etsi verbis exprimere vix possumus, possibile tamen esse Deo cogitatione per fidem illustratâ assequi possumus, et constantissime credere debemur." S. Concil. Trid. sess. xiii. c. 1.

And therefore, in contemplating the history of the Holy See, and of the line of Pontiffs who unite us with the Presence of the Incarnate Word manifested on earth, and also with the Sovereignty of the same Lord now reigning at the right hand of God, sense and reason have their proper sphere; but there is a sanctuary into which they cannot enter, and a presence which determines all, and is the substance and the life of the whole supernatural fact, of which Faith alone has cognizance.

Now, as this appears to me to be the particular truth which the progression of human error has at this day especially assailed, and as it seems also that our Divine Lord, who at other times has been pleased, to use the language of men, to accept the battle with the perverse will and perverted reason of man,—sometimes on one side of His indivisible truth, and sometimes on another; in one age upon His Godhead coequal with the Father, in another upon His true and proper manhood taken from His Immaculate Mother; now upon the mystery of the Altar, which most nearly represents the action and proportions of His Incarnation; and now upon the whole order and action of His Church upon the world;—so now at last, it would seem, for reasons partly, no doubt, as yet inscrutable, but partly even at this time, already most evident, He has accepted the whole combat upon one point, the key and centre of all His supernatural action among men, namely, on the Sovereign Pontificate of His Vicar upon earth.

It is needless to point out how, in this one truth, all are contained; how the whole order, constitution, office, and endowments of the Church are summed up, concentrated, perpetuated, and exercised by its Head; how, without its Head, the Body would cease to cohere, that is, to exist; and how, in the existence and action of the Church, the whole Faith, with its aureola of theology around it, and the action of sacramental grace, with all its laws of divine precision, are vitally contained and manifested to the world. It was no exaggeration of St. Ambrose to say, "Ubi Petrus, ibi Ecclesia;" nor of St. Avitus, "If the Pope of the City (*i.e.* of Rome) be called into doubt, it is no Bishop, but the Episcopate at once, which will be seen to waver." *

And if the subject of the Sovereign Pontificate be essentially and in itself vital to the Church and to the Faith, certainly it is one which ought to be in the front of our teaching. I think I may say that if there be a subject which fulfils all the tests, both

---

* "Si Papa Urbis vocatur in dubium, Episcopatús jam videbitur, non Episcopus, vacillari."—Bibl. Max.—Gallandii tom. x.—St. Aviti Ep. xxxi.

general and particular, of what is seasonable and necessary in this land and at this moment, it is that which, arising a few years ago no larger than " a man's foot," and despised then, as the extravagance of Canonists or the dream of Theologians, and thrust aside by the boastful confidence of Protestantism, and denounced by politicians, and derided by the thousand tongues of public opinion, has risen and spread until it has overcast the whole of Europe as the one ultimate and critical question of our state and time. Not only do we, as Catholics, perceive that in it is summed up the whole presence of the supernatural order, but even men of the world have likewise become aware that the whole natural order of political society, as it has hitherto existed in Christendom, is tied by this single keystone. They know as well as we that the political question of the day is not between degrees of more or less in the same order, but between two social systems: the old, which created Christendom; and the new, which let loose the Revolution. The most antipapal, anti-catholic, and antichristian among us does not affect to deny that the whole order of Christian society in Europe arose from the action of the Church, and therefore of its Head, upon the nations of the world.

With a lively sense that so great a matter ought

to have fallen into stronger and better hands, I will endeavour to mark out what I hope may indicate at least the line and the divisions of this vast subject.

And here I would lay down three principles which are of vital importance in treating of the Temporal Sovereignty of the Holy See.

1. The first is, never to lose sight for a moment of the supernatural character of the subject matter. It is not so much the stratagem of the antagonists of this day, for they know no better, but their inevitable necessity, that, having lost faith in the supernatural, they must themselves treat, and challenge or invite us also to treat, the subject of the Sovereign Pontificate in the order of history, that is, on the mere level of nature. We can consent so to deal with it in so far as we might also deal with the fact of the Incarnation or of the Holy Eucharist in the order of nature. But in these and in the Supreme Pontificate there is, as I have said, a supernatural element, which not only refuses the test and the treatment of the natural order, but so predominates over the whole subject, as the greater over the less, and as the substance over the accessories, that all such treatment becomes partial, inadequate, and useless. This I shall hope to explain hereafter.

2. The second principle is, to bear in mind that, in dealing with the historical evidences of this subject, it is necessary not only to examine the several and detailed facts, but to collect and to appreciate the whole *cumulus* of the evidences in one view. They who have been used to examine the historical proofs of the most certain events and facts—such as the succession of monarchies, the lives and actions of the most notorious men, as well as such vital matters as the canonicity of inspired Books, and the extrinsic evidence of the Christian revelation—well know that the evidence arising from the summing-up of all its detailed proofs is distinct from them all, and forms a separate and higher kind of proof, both convincing and persuasive. Such is eminently the case here; as we shall see, on finally collecting into one focus all the lights of history which surround the path and the presence of the Pontificate and the Sovereignty of the Vicars of Jesus Christ.

3. The third principle is, always to maintain the indivisible unity of the subject; and as we refuse to treat it in the natural order alone, so never to distinguish, except in thought, the Pontificate and the Sovereignty Spiritual and Temporal of the Vicariate of Jesus Christ. As in treating of human nature we may contemplate the body and the soul, the intellect and the will, the expansion of life in child-

hood, its wider range in youth, its sway and maturity in manhood, and yet we are only distinguishing without dividing the integral and inseparable perfections and properties of one individual life; so it is with the Sovereign Pontificate of the Vicars of Jesus Christ, whether contemplated lineally in the progressive manifestation of its prerogatives along the whole line of Pontiffs, or in the person of Pius IX., in whom all the inheritance of the Vicariate of the Son of God, both as Pontiff and as Sovereign, resides in full. It is one of the tactics of our adversaries to profess that they do not attack the Spiritual Supremacy, but only the Temporal Sovereignty of the Pope. By offering battle upon this ground, many are tempted to leave their true and sure position, and to give away, with their eyes shut, the key of their entrenchment, namely, that both the Spiritual and the Temporal, though given in different ways and at different times, are yet both gifts of the same Divine Lord, and both inhere at this time, by the Divine will, in the person of his Vicar. If it be conceivable that He should have given the one without the other, now that He has given both, it is not for us to conceive that they should be parted. The Sovereign Pontificate is conceivable to us only as God has manifested it. We receive its image from its manifestation. We have no other conception of it except as He has revealed it by His action upon the world. If it be said, We can conceive it as it once existed before the Temporal Power was known to this world; we answer, We may conceive it for that time, because God so manifested it then; we cannot conceive it for this, because God has manifested it otherwise now. But this manifestation is the will of God. We cannot conceive a retrogression in the works of God; as if His Church, the tree of Life, should fall into decay and cast its branches. We know it as God has matured it. We have no better reason to conceive of the Church now as it was in the Catacombs, than to conceive it as it was in the synagogue or in the wilderness. The works and the ways of God are onward to perfection; "sine pœnitentia enim sunt dona et vocatio Dei,"* "the gifts and the calling of God are without repentance." To us the Spiritual and the Temporal Powers of the Supreme Pontiff have gradually become integral and inseparable ideas in the same divine order and creation.

In this sense, then, the Temporal Sovereignty of the Supreme Pontiff is of divine institution. It was inherent in the Pontificate, which was conferred by a direct act of our Divine Lord; it was called out into

* Rom. xi. 29.

exercise by Divine providence as soon as Christendom arose; it has been confirmed and sustained by the same Divine providence over its local territory for more than a thousand years. In this sense, then, it is divine; and though not necessary in any absolute way to the spiritual office of the Church, which for centuries accomplished itself without a territory, it is necessary to the perfect and peaceful discharge of its mission to the world. When we see that the Divine predestination has willed it, and the Divine providence has constituted it, we are unable to contemplate it in any other light than that of the Divine will; or to regard it in any way but as, next to the institution of the Church on earth, the creation which is most visibly and emphatically divine in its origin, character, and operation.

The Pontificate and the Sovereignty of the Vicar of Jesus Christ was fully and perfectly, that is, either actually or potentially, conferred upon the person of St. Peter in the moment when he received of the Son of God the keys of the kingdom of heaven. The whole power of supernatural government, with all its principles, prerogatives, and sanctions, was conveyed to him by that one act of investiture. No new accessions have been made to it; no further grants or enlargements of jurisdiction have been bestowed upon him or upon his successors. It has, indeed, required a succession of two hundred and fifty Pontiffs to bring forth and to exercise all the fulness of this original commission. If the Apostle does not hesitate to call the Church by the name of Christ,* I need not fear to draw a parallel between the unfolding of the mystery of the Incarnation in the Person of Jesus from the moment of the Annunciation to the hour of the Ascension, and the progressive manifestation of His Priesthood and His Royalties in the person of His Vicar upon earth. Two points of precise analogy exist in this parallel. First, the full and perfect presence of these two supernatural facts from the first moment of their constitution; and next, the progressive manifestation and exercise of their power in the order of time and of events.

Now the spiritual mission of the Church, and the state of the heathen world, demanded by strict necessity that the Spiritual Supremacy and Pontificate of the Vicars of Jesus Christ should be first exercised, and therefore be first manifested to the nations and races of mankind.

It is not my intention, for it is not necessary, that I should offer proofs of the original plenitude of the Pontificate from the beginning of the Church. Nevertheless, what I purpose to offer will, I believe,

* 1 Cor. xii. 27.

be found to be a full and complete proof of what I may assume.

I would propose to any one, who either desires evidence or explicit illustration of this fact, to take as the two terms of his inquiry into this question, first, on the one extreme, the well-known passage of Eusebius, describing the attitude of St. Victor in the middle of the second century, in the Paschal controversy with the Asiatic Churches, and the intercession of St. Irenæus, praying the Roman Pontiff to refrain from the act of cutting them off by excommunication ($\dot{a}\pi o\kappa \acute{o}\pi \tau \epsilon \iota \nu$); together with the words of Tertullian, fifty years later, in which he rails with the wounded pride of a Montanist against the sovereign power which had already passed sentence on him. " Audio etiam edictum esse propositum, et quidem peremptorium, Pontifex scilicet Maximus, quod est Episcopus Episcoporum edicit, Ego,"* &c. And on the other extreme I would request him to place—no inconsiderable landmark—the twenty-one folio volumes of the *Bibliotheca Pontificia* of Roccaberti.

Now, what a forest of fifteen hundred years is to the first acorn which struck its root in the soil, in lineal descent, unity of substance, legitimacy of multiplication, identity of kind, continuity of exist-

* Tertull. de Pud. c. 1.

ence, maturity of nature, harmonious expansion, and perfect symmetry of structure, such is the Sovereign Pontificate of Roccaberti's one-and-twenty folios compared with that of Eusebius and Tertullian.

My object in this example is to point out one only fact, which will throw much light upon the subject properly before us.

What was it that, out of the simple fact described in the narrative of Eusebius and the invectives of Tertullian, elicited so vast a body of scientific and exact treatises on the Sovereign Pontificate? What defined and elevated it into a province of theology, and gave to it a definition among the doctrines of Christianity?

It needs no learning to answer, that this slow but vast process was the result of the antagonism which from Tertullian to Cerularius, from Cerularius to Huss, and from Huss to Luther, has demanded the exercise and expression of the Supreme Pontificate. The *Bibliotheca Pontificia* is the record and the summary, the retrospective estimate and the resulting expression, of this divine institution of supernatural power, as manifested by the antagonism which has unceasingly contended against the Vicars of Jesus Christ.

Now any one who will turn over the volumes of Roccaberti will perceive at once that they are almost exclusively filled with treatises upon the Spiritual Supremacy of the Sovereign Pontiffs. The subject of the Temporal Power comes in most sparingly, and, as it were, incidentally, by the way. I doubt if there be one whole treatise on this subject. A chapter extracted from the larger treatises of Dominicus Soto and of Bellarmine, a passage from Stapleton, and one fuller treatment of the subject by Suarez, constitutes nearly all that is to be found in a direct or substantive form throughout the one-and-twenty volumes. How are we to account for this fact? And what are we to infer from it?

The answer does not appear to me to be difficult to find.

I would venture to reply, that as in science, so also in theology, and in the history of every truth, certain periods are to be traced: first, the period of conception; secondly, of definition; and lastly, of application and of scientific manifestation. It appears to be the will and order of the Divine Head of the Church, that the Spiritual Sovereignty of His Vicar should be first exercised and resisted, affirmed and denied, contested and defined; and that without the schisms of the East and West the *Bibliotheca Pontificia* would not as yet have reached its completion.

And in this I seem to see a reason why as yet

the subject of the Temporal Power or prerogatives of the Supreme Pontiff are still waiting for a Bibliotheca. The *Regalia Petri* are now in turn the subject of a world-wide and unceasing antagonism. From generation to generation throughout the kingdoms of modern Europe, and especially wheresoever the poison of Machiavelli in the fifteenth century, and the anarchy of Protestantism in the sixteenth, has entered into political society, the main subject of jealous legislation, of railing controversy, and sometimes of more grave and respectable error, has been the position of Rome in Italy, and the Temporal Power of the Sovereign Pontiff. From which fact, so far from believing that the temporal prerogatives of the Vicar of Jesus Christ are entering on the period of their decline, I rather infer that they are already in the period of their fuller appreciation and manifestation. The materials of a Bibliotheca Pontificia have long been collecting; but the time of digesting and defining appears not even yet to be come. The line of Pontiffs from St. Gregory the Great to Pius IX. have vindicated and exercised the temporal prerogatives of their Pontificate; a host of theologians in all languages have defended and justified it; ten Councils, of which two are General, have recognised it; a multitude of lesser writers, during the last three hundred years, have treated it in its relation to modern society; and now at last, in the great Pontificate of our Holy Father, who is a Confessor for these prerogatives of the Holy See, the whole Episcopate of the universal Church has given, in all its tongues, an unanimous suffrage and testimony. The "magisterium juge Ecclesiæ" has spoken, as it only speaks in prelude of an authoritative definition.* All these things would lead us to expect anything rather than the disappearance from the face of the earth of a power to which the whole world, "some, indeed, even out of envy and contention, but some also for goodwill,"† are turning, as to the one object which fills the whole field of vision, the one presence which either sustains or obstructs the whole will of two great antagonist arrays. It is surely not paradoxical rather to say that this is the period of the manifestation and justification of the Temporal Power of the Sovereign Pontiffs; that what the Arian period was to the doctrine of the Holy Trinity, and the Protestant period to the doctrine of justification, such the present period is to the full manifestation of the Supreme Pontificate in its twofold relations to the spiritual and political order of the world.

* This great authority has already become a rule to govern the judgment of Ecclesiastical bodies.
† Philipp. i. 15.

Inasmuch as it is better to err by excess of caution than by defect of explicitness, I will here say what I must ask all Catholics to pardon as needless to them, but necessary perhaps for those that are without.

In the parallel I have drawn between the gradual definition of the doctrines of the Holy Trinity and of the Immaculate Conception, and the subject of the Temporal Power of the Sovereign Pontiffs, I have in no way and in no sense expressed or implied that the Temporal Power constitutes the material object of a dogma of Faith.

The first of the two conditions of a dogma of Faith is, that it was revealed by God to the Apostles.

The local sovereignty of the Vicar of our Lord over Rome and the Marches was a fact in Providence many centuries afterwards, and as such can form no proper or direct matter of a dogma of Faith. The instinct of a Catholic child would perceive this; and Catholics will forgive my pointing it out only for the sake of those who either have not the light of faith, or who are given to the spirit of contention.

Nevertheless, the Temporal Sovereignty affords abundant and proper matter for a definition, or judgment, or authoritative declaration of the Church, like the disciplinary decrees of General Councils, or, finally, the authoritative sentences in the Bulls of Pontiffs—as, for instance, in the Bull *Auctorem fidei*—of which many relate to discipline, to ecclesiastical and mixed questions bearing on temporal things.

And to such an authoritative utterance, under anathema, and by the voice of the whole Church through the Supreme Pontiff, the subject of the Temporal Power of the Vicar of Jesus Christ may legitimately, and not improbably, attain; and such a *judicium ecclesiæ*, or authoritative sentence, would be binding on the consciences of all the faithful, and the contrary would be noted as "propositio falsa, juribus Concilium Generalium et summorum Pontificum læsiva, scandalosa, et schismati fovens."*
And yet the subject matter may not be among the original articles of revealed doctrine, but of the nature of a dogmatic fact attaching to a Divine doctrine and institution, viz., the Vicariate of St. Peter and his successors; and therefore, after declaration, it would be of incontrovertible certainty and universal obligation, so that the denial of it would involve grave sin.

That I may make this progressive manifestation more evident, I would briefly draw out the periods

* In Bulla "Auctorem fidei," 74.

through which the Temporal Sovereignty of the Vicars of Jesus Christ appears to have passed towards its present form.

1. It is self-evident that the Temporal Sovereignty of the Popes is a power relative to Christian peoples and princes, forasmuch as it is by baptism and regeneration alone that men, and therefore nations, become subjects of the Church. In the first period of three hundred years, while as yet the civil powers of the world were pagan, these prerogatives of the Vicars of Christ had no subject matter for their exercise. They existed in the plenitude of their office; but they were related to an order to be afterwards created. They were inherent, as the sacramental power resides in the priest to whom no "*materia apta*" for consecration is present, or as the habitual power of absolution while as yet he has no jurisdiction over souls.

It is therefore vain and senseless to quote examples of obedience in the Pontiffs to heathen emperors and to a heathen senate, as a proof of their obligations towards Christian princes and Christian legislatures. By the grace of Christianity Christian princes and legislators stand to the Church in other and higher relations than the heathen. If they would claim with the heathen, they renounce their Christianity. Doubtless the Pontiffs would act towards heathen powers now as the Pontiffs acted then; but no Christian prince, or people, can claim the obedience exacted by the heathen without apostasy from the Christian name. This first period, then, was one not of sovereignty or order, but of patience and of martyrdom, and is no precedent and gives no principles.

2. The second period may be called the period of liberation. To the least discerning it must be manifest that God had some purpose of His divine wisdom in the migration of Constantine and of the Empire from Rome to Byzantium. What could be more improbable than that an emperor should forsake the imperial city of a thousand years; or that a Christian prince should, in the very fervour of his conversion, depart from the Vicar of Jesus Christ? Surely it was in the Divine Will to show to the world that His Church has no need of human support; that the stone "cut out without hands," * "without hands" also was to fill the whole earth; and likewise to reveal, by a melancholy history of ambition, heresy, tyranny, and schism, to what a Christian people, by disobedience to the Vicars of His Son, may fall.

But this is too large a subject. It is enough for our present purpose to point out that the migration

* Dan. ii. 34.

of the Empire was an abandonment of Rome and of Italy. The Emperors ceased to be lords by occupation; they ceased to exercise the duties, and therefore the rights, of sovereigns; they could no longer even defend Rome against the Barbarian invasions; probably, to buy them off from attacking Constantinople, they connived at their irruptions into Italy. If, as Aristotle says, property consists in the κτῆσις καὶ χρῆσις, in the possession and the use of anything, then the Byzantine Emperors ceased to be proprietors of Italy and of Rome. Nay more, they lost their rights, not only by abandonment, but by abuse, by tyranny, by heresy, by schism, by persecution, by the meanest vexation, and by the guilt of assassination, attempted even against the person of the Pontiffs, as in the case of St. Martin I., of Sergius, and of Gregory II.

Now the abandonment of Rome was the liberation of the Pontiffs. Whatsoever claims to obedience the Emperors may have made, and whatsoever compliance the Pontiff may have yielded, the whole previous relation, anomalous, and annulled again and again by the vices and outrages of the Emperors, was finally dissolved by a higher power. The providence of God permitted a succession of irruptions, Gothic, Lombard, and Hungarian, to desolate Italy, and to efface from it every remnant of the Empire. The Pontiffs found themselves alone; the sole fountains of order, peace, law, and safety. And from the hour of this providential liberation, when, by a Divine intervention, the chains fell off from the hands of the successor of St. Peter, as once before from his own, no sovereign has ever reigned in Rome except the Vicar of Jesus Christ. The moral import of this Divine action must be adequately appreciated. It cancelled, abolished, and extinguished finally and for ever the right of conquest, possession, occupation, and property claimed by the Emperors over Italy and Rome. The throne of sovereignty was vacant by the visitation of God. It reverted to its primitive rights as a virgin soil, the title and inheritance of which is inherent in the people who possessed it by birth, by toil, and by burial. They once more became and assumed the style of the Roman Republic. It has been argued, with great learning and apparent reason, by a distinguished Italian writer,* that the Roman Senate was always the true and legitimate sovereignty; and that as the presence of the Empire did not constitute, so neither did the translation of the Empire diminish, the rights of the Senate in Rome. There existed, therefore, the full and independent popular sovereignty of the Roman people in all its material

* Troya. See Civiltà Cattolica, quad. 265, p. 53.

completeness, lacking only form and manifestation in the person whom it should invest with its execution.

3. The interval between the failure of the Empire in Italy and the confirmation of the Temporal Sovereignty of the Pontiffs was an *interregnum*.

4. Nor was it of long duration. In the three hundred years before the translation of the Empire a power had grown up far more imperial over the reason and will of man than the iron despotism of the Roman. It had pervaded the intelligence of men with truth, and their hearts with a law of life. It had subdued them by convictions of the reason and persuasions of the moral nature, and won to itself the whole confidence and attachment of their will, with all its freedom and powers. And this interior and supernatural power of direction and government over the actions and hearts of men flowed from one centre, and was embodied in one person, the Bishop of Rome. On him devolved, by the inevitable operation of a moral and political necessity, the chief authority to sustain, protect, and uphold the broken and abandoned social order of Rome and Italy. The floods which swept all other authorities away threw out into bolder relief and more conspicuous prominence the Supreme Pastoral authority of the Vicars of Jesus Christ. To whom

else should the people go? for they alone had not only the words of eternal life, but the sole and supreme moral power to support and to reorganise the shattered society of Rome. Political necessity, which is the highest natural law in human society (forasmuch as it is the voice and the finger of Divine Providence), pointed to the successors of St. Peter as the only judges, lawgivers, and protectors of the people. They were the saviours of the city and of the Roman republic. I forbear to narrate, what all will at once remember, how this was literally verified in St. Leo the Great, and in others. It is no figure of speech, but a strict historical event.

Now, by all the laws which govern the political changes of governments and people, if the Pontiffs had put forth their hands to take the sovereign power which was thus laid upon them, they might most justly have done so. All laws, human and divine, would have confirmed and consecrated their act. But they did not so. It was thrust upon them, and they put it from them. Like as our Divine Lord, when He saw that the people would come to take Him and make Him a King, fled into the mountain Himself alone,* so His Vicars declined the character of sovereignty, and lamented the distrac-

* St. John vi. 15.

tions and burdens of their secular care. Such was their state from the fifth to the seventh century. It was the political necessity of saving an abandoned and afflicted people from sufferings by war, by famine, by pestilence, of which the world has no parallel either for intensity or duration, that first invested the Roman Pontiffs with what has been well described as "a Sovereign Prefecture, and the Dictatorship of a Father." *

5. And here we meet with a new and still more explicit title to the sovereignty of Rome,—the express demand, suffrage, and vote of the people. It will be observed that this election was not the hasty and turbulent act of an intimidated and menaced population, drilled and driven to poll-booths in a crisis of excitement, and with the precipitate violence of a revolution and an invasion at their back; but the calm, prolonged, spontaneous, and deliberate action of many successive generations, all conspiring for ages in the one ardent desire to shelter themselves and their children under the sovereignty of the Roman Pontiffs. It would be too long to transcribe the evidences of this fact. It will be enough to remind you of the words of St. Leo the Great, who excused himself to the Empress Pulcheria for not leaving Rome, because "the cha-

* Civiltà Cattolica, quad. 262, p. 446.

rity he bore to the public safety, and the prayers of the citizens, who would have risen tumultuously and in despair at his departure, prevented him;"* and, again, of the popular rising in Rome, in Ravenna, and in the whole of Italy, to protect Pope Sergius from an attempted assassination; or, again, of the devotion of both the Romans and the Lombards, who surrounded Gregory II., to protect his person against the Emperor Leo the Isaurian; or of the union of the Duchies of Spoleto and Benevento, to protect Gregory III. against the attacks of Luitprand; or of Pope Zachary, who for ten years ruled over Rome beloved by the people, who under his government lived, as we read, "in magnâ securitate et lætitiâ;" or of Pope Stephen II., who, when he returned from France after the alliance of Quiersy with Pepin, was received by the people of Rome with the salutation, "Pater noster, et post Dominum salus nostra." For three hundred years before this event the Pontiffs had reigned supreme over the political and social order of Rome; and that not only without opposition or jealousy from the people, but with a long tradition of loving and grateful attachment. Of which no better expression can be found than in the letter of the Roman people to Pepin, in which the Senate and the whole

* S. Leo M., ep. xxvii. 4.

people of Rome declare themselves as follows: "We are the firm and faithful servants of the Holy Church of God, and of the thrice-blessed Prelate, your spiritual Father in the Gospel, our Lord, Paul, Supreme Pontiff and universal Pope, because he is our Father and best of Pastors, who ceases not daily to toil and contend for our safety, as did also his brother of holy memory, our most blessed Lord Pope Stephen."

I will add only one more fact. In the life of Pope Adrian, given by Anastasius, we read that the people of Spoleto and Rieti, and all the rest of the Duchy of Spoleto, "ardently desired (*ardenter desideravére*) to deliver themselves over to the service of Blessed Peter and the Holy Roman Church. But fearing their king" (that is, the Lombard invader Desiderius), "they dared not to do so." Wherefore, after he had been overthrown by Charlemagne at Chiuse, "confestim, generaliter ad præfatum almificum Pontificem confluentes advenerunt," "immediately and in a body they came in streams from every side to the forenamed merciful Pontiff,"—"ejusque provoluti pedibus obnixe sanctam ipsius ter beatitudinem deprecati sunt, ut eos in servitio B. Petri Sanctæque ejus Romanæ Ecclesiæ susciperet, et more Romanorum tonsurari faceret,"*—

* Civiltà Cattolica, quad. 265, p. 66.

"and, prostrate at his feet, urgently prayed his Holiness to receive them into the service of Blessed Peter and his Holy Roman Church, and to order them to be tonsured after the manner of the Romans." And finally, the people of Istria, in like manner, fled for refuge to the Pontiff, praying him to afford them "redemptionem et protectionem a Deo et B. Petro per vestram Apostolicam dispositionem." *

With these facts before us, which are but a handful gleaned from the abundant field of the four centuries from the translation of the Empire to the formal manifestation of the Temporal Sovereignty of the Pontiffs, it is abundantly evident that while the Divine Will declared itself by the two great facts of the liberation of the Popes from all civil subjection, and by the political necessity which, whether they would or no, clothed them with the attributes, if it did not also confer the name, of Sovereignty, the will also of the people of Rome and of Italy declared itself with a deliberation, a persistence, and a uniformity which rendered it imperative and inevitable that the Prefecture and Dictatorship of the Pontiffs should become in name, what the providence of God had already made it in fact, a true and proper Sovereignty.

And here I cannot forbear, in passing, to point

* Civiltà Cattolica, quad. 265, p. 67.

out the fact that the invasions of the Lombards were with the avowed intention of forming a united Italy, under their own northern sovereignty; and that the main obstacle and chief object of their ambition was Rome. The intervention of Charlemagne put an end to the Barbarian invasions, and to the experiments at an armed Italian unity, renewed, from time to time, by the Emperors of Germany, and now in our days by Sardinia. The situation, as the phrase is, has nothing new in it, and its issue bids fair, in the end, to be the same.

After the restitution by Pepin and Charlemagne of the states which the Lombards had usurped, the Pontiffs Stephen III. and St. Leo III. exercised the most explicit power of sovereignty, in creating them Patricians of Rome, a civil office deriving its existence from the Pontiffs. In afterwards consecrating Charlemagne to the Empire, St. Leo did not extinguish his own independence, nor create one superior to himself.

6. To this must be added further, that which is held to be an axiom in jurisprudence,—the right arising from possession. It would not be an adequate appreciation of this fact if we were to date it only from the period of its peaceful confirmation under Pepin and Charlemagne. The possession of the Pontiffs commences with the abandonment of

Rome by the Emperors; and the abandonment by the Emperors begins not from the time when they ceased to claim it, as our kings claimed the kingdom of France for centuries after they had lost all possession, but from the time when they ceased to exercise the highest of a sovereign's duties—that of protection. Many generations must pass away, many old traditions must wear out, many customs of thought and language must become obsolete, and many claims once valid must by desuetude become pretensions, before the Empire could become extinct in Italy. It took ages to strike its roots, and ages to pull them up again. No human agency could have so soon brought it to pass that the Empire of Rome should vanish away, as if it had never been. Its complete dethronement is visibly the work of God. From the time, then, which may be put, at latest, in the age of St. Leo the Great, the Pontiffs have been the only rulers in Rome. Fourteen hundred years of possession, reaching not only beyond all royalties in the world, but beyond even the existence of Christian Europe, confirms the title of Sovereignty in the Vicars of Jesus Christ. The Count de Maistre, with his wonderful felicity of expression, has said, "There is not a sovereignty in Europe more easily to be justified, if I may use the word, than that of the Sovereign

Pontiffs. It is like the Law of God, *justificata in semetipsâ.*" *

Such, then, are its successive epochs: first, its liberation from all civil subjection; secondly, its passive occupation of the abandoned government of Rome; thirdly, the political necessity which forced its exercise upon the Pontiffs; fourthly, the free suffrage and election of the people, conscious of its benign and beneficent protection; and finally, the unbroken possession of more than a thousand years.

I have thus far endeavoured to treat this question as one of evidence and of history, and therefore within the jurisdiction of sense and of reason. But I cannot consent to treat the Temporal Sovereignty of the Vicars of Jesus Christ in the light of the natural order alone, as the history of the Califate or of the twelve Cæsars. There is a supernatural element in the subject, never for a moment to be eliminated. The creation and existence of Christendom, that is, of the mixed and complex spiritual and civil order of Christian nations, is a part of the predestination of God; and God, who willed it, has also accomplished it; and, in accomplishing it, has employed the instrument which He had prepared for that end, the Pontificate of the Vicar of His Incarnate Son. The Temporal

* Du Pape, l. ii. c. 6.

prerogatives of the Pontificate are the divine conditions whereby the Christian order of this world has been created and sustained.

It is therefore neither reasonable nor possible to discuss the question of the Temporal Sovereignty as if it were a mere accident of the Spiritual Supremacy, not united with it in the first centuries, and separable from it now. What was united in the predestination of God may not be separated in the speculations of men. It seems also to betray a superficial apprehension of the work of the kingdom of God upon earth, to confine its action to individuals, and to exclude it from the sphere of government, legislation, law, public order, social progress, and from the direction of nations, races, peoples, and the organised and continuous life of human society. I can see little signs of depth, or reflection, or maturity, or comprehensiveness in such reasonings. Neither can I find any evidence of spiritual intuition, or of illumination, in those who can discover from the history we have been reviewing no higher sentiment in the Christian peoples of Rome and Italy than a desire to shelter themselves under a rich and easy, or a merely powerful and successful, ruler. There was assuredly a profounder instinct and a more supernatural impulse moving them to cast themselves at the feet of the Vicar of Jesus Christ, and praying him to be their king. It is the reversal of the sin of those who clamoured to the Lord for a king like the other nations. Of them the Lord said to the Prophet, "They have not rejected thee, but Me, that I should not reign over them." * So would He say to His Pontiffs, "They have not chosen thee, but they have chosen Me, that I should reign over them." If the Jewish people cried, "Non habemus regem nisi Cæsarem,"† the Christian people answered, "Non habemus regem nisi Christum." ‡ In voluntarily subjecting themselves to His Vicar, they chose Him for their King. Faith in the Incarnation would inspire this choice, and devotion to the presence of the Incarnate Word, in the person of His Vicar, would make the inspiration a dictate of the conscience and of the heart. It was the common sense of the faithful which moved them to place themselves under the government of one who governed in the name and by the laws of the Divine Redeemer of mankind. Is it wonderful that the people of Italy fled from the Pharaos of Constantinople to the "Pontifices almificos," meekest rulers upon earth? In so doing they sought not only a political justice, but the most intimate relation they could attain to

---

* 1 Kings viii. 7.   † St. John xix. 15.
‡ St. Iren. iv. 21.

the person of their unseen Lord and Judge: they had made trial of imperial decrees, and in exchange they sought for the equity, stability, and clemency of the Evangelical Law. They sought the sovereignty of the Pontiffs, not only for reasons of a natural prudence, but of a supernatural faith, believing that of all sovereigns they would be the most just and benign, and of all legislation, that of the Vicars of Christ would be the most pure and beneficent to individuals and to society. They knew them to be the guides of men in the way of eternal life, and the guardians and expositors of the only law of peace. Faith and love towards the Divine Redeemer of mankind taught them to desire to be the subjects of the only person who ruled supremely in His name. This I conceive to be the ultimate title of the Temporal Power of the Sovereign Pontiffs over the people whom God had providentially enabled to place themselves under their rule and protection.

And this is a principle pregnant with great moral truths. For certainly such a popular election as this, so free and so deliberate, so illuminated in prudence natural and supernatural, and so governed by the highest instincts of faith in the revelation and will of God, is not to be revoked by a sedition, or by a rebellion, or by any act of the popular will less in kind or lower in its moral dignity than that which in the beginning elicited and formed it. If the original election was a great popular act of faith, how shall the revocation of it be less than a commensurate act of popular impiety? The Sovereignty of the Pontiffs cannot be dissolved by the popular vote, like the sovereignties of France and England. Revolutions against our princes violate the constitution; but a revolution against the Vicar of Jesus Christ is a violation of high and deep instincts of Christianity. It may be even lawful and justifiable to be weary of Stuarts or of Capets; but it cannot be either lawful or sinless to be weary of the Vicar of Jesus Christ. With us a revolution might be a just impatience of unlawful acts; with the subjects of the Vicar of Christ it must be a "tædium de Deo." For let it not be said that such a revolution can be justified by a political necessity, or by the law of social self-defence; for it would be an easy task to show that no Pontiff, in all the line from St. Peter to Pius IX., has ever given cause for a just resistance of his subjects, or has ever, in his civil government, violated the laws of his state, or the relations between him and his people. Yet such a cause as this alone can clear a revolution of the sin of rebellion before God. And rebellion against the Vicar of the Incarnate Word is in the same order as the rejection of his Master. The question, then, is not between two dynasties, or two princes, or two political constitutions; but between the natural and supernatural societies; between the civilisation of the mere human will, and the civilisation which is perfected and sustained by grace. Christian society sprung from the revealed faith and law of God. It was moulded by the unity of the Church, inspired and tied, as with a keystone, by the Pontificate of the Vicars of Jesus Christ. When political society revolts from him, it revolts also from the Faith, the Law, the Sacraments, and the Supremacy of the Church of God. Witness all Protestant countries; witness also the inchoate schisms of Portugal and Sardinia. Civilisation in revolt from the Christian Church is Christian only by accident, or by lingering tradition, or in name; in its essence and principle it is mere natural society, the creature of the human will, in the order of nature alone. To what social and political disorder such a people must descend, the religious conflicts, and the history of divorce in Germany, America, and England, suffice to show. To this state also Italy, goaded on by England, seems passionately bent on reducing itself..

The latest and perhaps the most considerable example of the fallacy of treating the question of the Temporal Sovereignty of the Pope on the basis of the mere national order, is to be found in a recent pamphlet, *L'Empereur, Rome, et le Roi d'Italie.*

The writer argues that all nations have from God the power of disposing of themselves by their own free will; that the Temporal Power of the Pope rests upon their free choice, and that they are competent to retract what once they gave; that to deny this would be to declare them " adscripti glebæ," and therefore slaves; that the argument used by the Spanish Government, that Rome belongs not to the Romans, but to the Catholics throughout the world, disfranchises and expatriates the Romans, and reduces them to slavery.

Now to those who deny the Christian and Catholic order in the world, this argument may have its force. To those who believe in the Divine institution of the Catholic Church, and the creation of Christian Europe, it has little. If we believe that God has instituted His kingdom upon earth, and fixed the head and centre of it in Rome, as of old in Jerusalem, it is God Himself who by His divine action has taken Rome out of this category of mere natural societies. He has conferred upon the Romans a trust, a privilege, a prerogative, a glory, far above all people. He has elevated even their natural state to a supernatural condition and office. In the early centuries they so well perceived this truth, that they freely chose the Pontiffs as their sovereigns. The lower order ascended into the higher: it was not absorbed, but perfected in it. It is neither expatriation nor slavery to be the subjects of a person who bears the Vicariate of the Redeemer of mankind; neither is it disfranchisement to deny to the caprice of individuals, encouraged and goaded by sedition, and armed with violence, both the right and the power to revoke and undo what the deliberate and unanimous wills of ages and generations accomplished. If I may reverently use the illustration, in the Person of our Divine Lord the Humanity became sacred by union with His Godhead. It lost none of its perfection by having no human personality; rather, its very perfection is in this, that humanity became divine, and was elevated above its own to a higher order. The liberty and perfection of our manhood in all its powers and functions were secured and sustained by this union and elevation. To claim for it a human independence, would be to reduce it from the divine to the natural order. So of the people whom He has chosen to be the guardians of the throne of the Vicar of His Incarnate Son. They once knew their true glory, which was equally their true interest. They once chose it by the most perfect and illuminated act of the popular will, under a visible and direct leading of the providence of God. It is waste of words to urge, that the most perfect administration of the Christian law cannot cross or prejudice the social or political welfare of a people, and that the most perfect administration of the Christian law is to be found in the action of the Supreme Pontiffs, not only upon their own subjects, but also upon the world. I can conceive no ground on which they can claim to rescind this act of God's providence and this wise election of their forefathers, but the assumption that the Christian law is at variance with social prosperity; or that the Christian law is not duly administered by the Vicar of Jesus Christ; or that the Pontiffs have violated not only the Christian law, but political justice, by acts of tyranny. The two first are absurd; the last is demonstrably false. We may boldly challenge them to allege an act in the whole history of the Pontiffs which would clear revolution against the Temporal Power from the guilt of rebellion.

The people of the Roman States, therefore, are neither expatriated nor enslaved by being called to a higher mission and office than other nations, but rather by failing to recognise their elevation and their dignity. By this they expatriate themselves of the highest citizenship, and enslave themselves to the lowest conditions of political revolution.

Deeply as every Catholic must deplore the continual advance of these disorders, driven onwards by the power of prejudice, which reigns absolute in the public opinion of England, no success, victory, or triumph can cause us more than a transient suffering, except only for the souls that perish in this warfare against the Vicar of our Lord. Again and again these floods of evil have swept over the Holy See. It has been submerged for a moment, and has risen again resplendent and powerful as before. The weakness of God is stronger than men. Though natural society, with the tide and impetuosity of four hundred years of departure from God, precipitate itself upon the Pontificate of Jesus Christ, we believe that it will stand when the kingdom of Italy, and the empires of France and Britain, will be a mere epoch in history, taught to children in a Christian world, to which Europe, though it be the centre, will be but a point of space. The writers and readers of newspapers believe us to be out of date and behind our time. The boastful and contemptuous civilisation of the 19th century cannot so much as perceive that which to us is the only vital element of the question. For this reason they are incapable of comprehending the attitude and conduct of the Holy Father in this long crisis.

During his Pontificate of fifteen years Pius the

Ninth has borne the assault of the whole tide of revolution. It is a majestic spectacle, which reminds us of the Temptation of his Master. Every form of compromise, concession, and traffic has been proposed to the Vicar of Jesus Christ to induce him to betray his divine and providential trust. The twofold Sovereignty committed to him is the type, embodiment, and guarantee of the Christian social order, and of the consecration of the civil powers of the world. To separate them would be to desecrate the government of nations. And therefore it is that the whole weight of the assault, both by force and by feint, is made upon this point alone. The Vicar of Jesus Christ is the living witness of the consecration of the civil powers to the law and kingdom of God. He holds, as it were, the divine principle in his person. If only he could be induced to give it away, the civil power of the world would descend to the order of nature. Therefore it is that all who desire to exclude the action and supremacy of the Christian faith and of the Christian Church from the sphere of government, aim at the overthrow of the Temporal Power of the Pope. Therefore, after railing upon the obstinacy of Pius IX. in the presence of danger, they have endeavoured to lure him to a compromise by the visions of an Italian Confederation under his presidency, or of "a free Church in a free State," with guarantees for his person and his purely spiritual authority. "All these things will I give thee, if, falling down, thou wilt adore me."* The Vicar of Jesus Christ knows too well the trust committed to him, the sacredness of his twofold sovereignty, and the mind of his Master, to yield a jot or a tittle of his prerogatives. To lose them by force would be simply spoliation, which would be endured once more, as often already before; but to give them away would be to betray his divine commission, and to throw down what the providence of God has built up. This is the true solution of the concentrated hostility and activity of the world against the Temporal Sovereignty of Pius IX. So long as the Vicar of Jesus Christ continues to be a Temporal Sovereign, the duty of all Temporal Rulers to consecrate their power by submission to the Christian faith and Christian law, is recorded in the public jurisprudence of the world, and inscribed upon the face of the earth. He sits as a Sovereign among Sovereigns, and as a Sovereign of higher jurisdiction, as the guardian of the Christian faith and law among the people of other sovereignties. It is an amiable but not a wise enthusiasm to say that, if he sat as an Apostle among Sovereigns, he would exert a greater power. As an Apostle only, the Vicar of

* St. Matt. iv. 9.

Jesus Christ never did, never could sit among Sovereigns as their judge. Would he sit there as the subject of any one of them, or of all together? And if he be not subject, he, *ipso facto*, becomes sovereign. The negation of subjection is the affirmation of Sovereignty. And therefore among the Sovereigns of the nations he presides as one over whom none has power, as one who has power over all; for to him is divinely committed the custody of the new law, and the judgment of all, whether princes or people, who by baptism are subjects of that law. And if he be Sovereign, then the possession of a sphere or territory within which to dwell is a necessity of logic and of fact. And the Divine Wisdom has foreseen this need, and the Divine Providence has supplied it. I say it is an amiable enthusiasm, because some who use this language love the Church well, and think to magnify its spiritual powers by using as a counsel of filial confidence the language which enemies use as a taunt. The enemies of the Holy Father are now taunting him to throw himself, like Hildebrand, upon his spiritual powers, and to become a great Pope by recognising and supplying what Europe in the nineteenth century demands. But the Vicar of Jesus Christ knows well enough what Europe in the nineteenth century demands. He knows that the days of St. Gregory VII. were not the days of Pius IX. He knows that the conflicts and the victories of St. Gregory VII. are incorporated in the conflicts and certain victories, whichsoever way the issue may be, of his own time; that he is still the guardian of the same law, which by heresy, schism, simony, spoliation, and divorce is violated now on a wider scale than in the eleventh century; and that, in conflict with the empires, kingdoms, legislatures, and nations of the world, it is his Sovereignty, recognised and venerated for a thousand years by the whole Christian world, which invests him with the traditional powers and rights, not only of remonstrance, but of judgment and of execution. His verdicts are solemn acts of Christendom, public events recognised in the jurisprudence of Europe, on which the eyes of the Christian world are set. None know this better than they who desire to dethrone the Vicar of Jesus Christ from this supremacy among Christian Princes; to destroy the power of the Church in the sphere of government; and to reduce it from a kingdom and sovereignty to a school of religious philosophy, and an association for charitable works.

I know full well that the argument which I have hitherto endeavoured to state is as powerless and as unintelligible to those who are without, as the supernatural element in the doctrine of the Holy

Eucharist, or of the mystical Body. How can they otherwise than gainsay what they neither believe nor understand? For this reason they invite us to discuss the question on their own level, and to place it among the problems of the natural order; for this reason, also, they are unable to comprehend the cumulus of proof on which as Catholics we confidently repose; for this cause, too, they invite us to divide the Temporal from the Spiritual Sovereignty, because they cannot apprehend the complex and ever-enlarging work of the Divine action through the Church upon the world. Some even of ourselves have at times been led to forget the obvious axioms with which we started, and have indulged in a kind of appeal to antiquity, that is, from the present mature and complex office of the Pontiffs to a supposed period of apostolical simplicity, when as yet Christendom had not been created. But God does not return upon His steps; and the Church, which is His manifestation upon earth, lives not in the past, but in the present, and her course is not backward on the dial, but onward to the fulness of time. If God predestinated Christendom, they who now imagine the Vicar of Christ divested of his Temporal Sovereignty, surely cannot read His divine providence. They turn backward from its conduct in the world. The destinies of the Church are, as yet, only in part revealed. It has accomplished its past, and it is working out its present mission to mankind. Its future we know not yet; but it will be accomplished, be that destiny and mission what it may, with the same divine certainty and unerring facility as in the past. It may be that the Vicars of Jesus Christ have only begun their toil and their tutelage of the monarchies and dynasties of princes and their royal houses; that a wider, larger, and weightier mission is before them to the nations and confederation of commonwealths, and to the wayward turbulence of the popular will. The Gospel of the Kingdom has not yet been preached to all nations. The Christian family has not yet assimilated to itself more than one-third of the human race. The leaven is in the meal, but it has, as yet, penetrated only a portion. We know that "the whole must be leavened." * The Christendom of to-day may be no more than the blade, or at most the stalk, to the full corn in the ear, which shall be hereafter. The Pontificate and the Sovereignty of the Vicars of Jesus Christ will then reign with their divine authority over a fold which shall enclose nations as yet neither Christian nor civilised, to which all the Christendom of the past is but as the first-fruits to the harvest. With

* St. Matt. xiii. 33.

what reason, then, do these admirers of antiquity propose to us that the Sovereign Pontiff should abdicate the manifold prerogatives which St. Gregory VII., St. Pius V., Benedict XIV., and Pius IX., have held in their hands to check or to guide the powers and movements of Christian monarchies and Christian nations, and should return to the patriarchal simplicity of St. Gregory the Great, reigning over the patrimonies of the Church, because as yet no Europe existed for him to guide and to sustain? Surely this implies no depth of insight and no breadth of knowledge, not only of the Christian, but even of the civil history of the world.

But it is time that I should bring this Preface to an end; and I know not how I can better sum up the purport of what I have said than by recording the words of one of the most apostolical pastors and most devoted princes of the Church, who was last year called from the midst of these perturbations to his eternal rest. In the summer of last year I had the happiness to see, though for the last time, the Cardinal Feretti, the much-loved kinsman of our Holy Father. It was at Porto d'Anzio, where he was awaiting the end of his lingering illness. He was speaking, with the faith of a Roman, and we may believe also with the prophetic light of a dying man, of the rising of the world against the Holy Father, and of the miseries which are falling upon the nations. But, he said: all will be for the furtherance of the Faith, and for the greater glory of the Holy See. By these very tumults and persecutions of the Vicar of Christ, "l orbe Cristiano diventera più Cattolico, e Roma più Pontificia," "the Christian world will become more Catholic, and Rome more than ever united to its Pontiffs."

St. Mary's, Bayswater,
  Feast of St. Charles, 1861.

PART FIRST.

The Origin of the Temporal Power.

LECTURE I.

"Let every soul be subject to higher powers: for there is no power but from God; and those that are, are ordained of God. Therefore, he that resisteth the power, resisted the ordinance of God. And they that resist, purchase to themselves damnation."—ROMANS xiii. 1, 2.

THESE words of the Apostle lay down a broad principle, which covers the constituted order of the whole world. There is no power but of God; the powers that be are ordained of God. I shall not, however, offer proof of this principle; for it is enough that we read it in Holy Writ. The Apostle applies this principle to a heathen empire, to a heathen prince, and to a Christian people; he commands the Christians of Rome to be subject to a heathen empire.

I intend to speak on the subject of the temporal power of the Holy Father, the Vicar of Jesus Christ. And in so doing, I shall take my point of departure from this broad principle, which the Holy Ghost by the Apostle has declared to the world, and has applied, as you have seen, to the case of a Christian people, and a heathen emperor. I do not intend to enter into any subtilties of theology, nor into the remote and complex legislation of the Church, nor into any large details of history. These three sources would, indeed, give me abundance of matter; but they would give more than I need; for I mean to treat this subject as simply and as practically as I can, to present it as far as is necessary to the intelligence, but chiefly to the conscience. I shall, therefore, confine myself strictly to three propositions, and to three consequences which follow from them.

The first proposition is this: that the temporal power of the Pope is ordained of God. The second: that the temporal power of the Pope has been the root, and the productive and sustaining principle of Christian Europe. And, thirdly: that the dissolution of the temporal power of the Pope would bring with it the dissolution of Christian Europe. And from these three propositions I shall draw three plain conclusions. The first is this: that he who resists the temporal power of the Pope, resists the ordinance of God. Secondly: that he who lends a hand or a tongue to the dissolution of that power, helps, so far as his hand or his tongue can, to the dissolution of Christian Europe. And thirdly: that he that does so will purchase judgment to himself. Which propositions, I think, fall within the limit of the words of St. Paul, speaking by the inspiration of God.

Now, these are days in which two things are eminently wanted among us. The first is an accurate and large knowledge of history. For anything more insular, partial, and incorrect than the histories of the Catholic Church which are in the hands of Englishmen is hardly to be found. It is remarkable that some of the most fair, impartial, and truthful histories of the Catholic Church, written of late years, have been written by persons who rejected the doctrines of Christianity, or at least were not members of the Church. For instance, in Germany, such writers as Ranke and Hurter; in France, Michelet, who renounced his faith, and Guizot; and in this country, such writers as Macaulay, Hallam, and the like. And yet these are not the books which are preferred by the people of this country. With a great avidity they read every anti-catholic history they can find, like Robertson, Gibbon, and works that retail their statements from them, in which are to be found nothing but a tradition of incorrect statements and misquoted authorities, handed from one to the other without so much as a verification of the text.

But there is something far more wanted among us still, and that is, first principles. For a man that reads history without first principles, is like a man that launches upon the sea without a compass. The lack of first principles is the main cause of the confusion which is around us. In these three lectures, then, I purpose to dwell chiefly on first principles; and I will assume, first, that you believe in the Incarnation; and next, that you believe in a visible Church which is the prolongation of the visible manifestation of the Incarnation. If any one does not hold these two propositions, some part of the argument which I shall use will perhaps be inapplicable; yet I believe that the greater part will be inevitable even to those who believe in nothing more than a Divine providence.

I. Now the first proposition on which I have to speak is this: that the temporal power of the Pope is ordained of God.

God has two ways in which He ordains the powers of the world—direct and indirect; direct by revealed interposition, indirect by Divine providence. I mean to show that the power of the Pope, spiritual and temporal, taken in its complex, is an ordinance partly direct, and partly indirect, and yet in both characters divine.

Now in proof of this proposition I may affirm, that our divine Lord Jesus Christ, being God and man, has in that twofold character all sovereignty in heaven and earth. As God from all eternity, and as Creator of the world, He is sovereign over all things He has made. But He has not only this eternal sovereignty, He has also a temporal sovereignty; and that temporal sovereignty began when the Son of God was incarnate, when the Eternal came into time, and became subject to the successions of time. Therefore, I would first observe here, that the distinction between spiritual and temporal is a secondary and less accurate one. The first true distinction is between eternal and temporal. The Son of God, then, has an eternal sovereignty as God; and He has also a temporal sovereignty as the incarnate God, because the eternal God entered into the sphere of time by incarnation. When He was manifested as God incarnate, the world was redeemed, and the laws of nature yielded to the pressure of His hand. When He wrought miracles, the sovereignty of the incarnate God was manifested. When He had redeemed the world, and when, as mediator, He ascended to His Father's throne, He was fully invested with the sovereignty purchased by His precious blood.

II. Again, this temporal sovereignty of the Son of God, that is, the sovereignty which He has over time and that which is done in time, and over the world and that which is in the world, again divides itself into two branches. First, into that which is natural; and secondly, into that which is supernatural. That branch of his temporal sovereignty which is in nature consists in His providence; for He who wrought miracles when He was visible in the world, continues invisibly, by the acts of His divine providence, to dispose all things. No one but a deist will, I think, deny this principle. The other branch of His temporal sovereignty is supernatural, and consists in the power which, by the Holy Ghost, from the day of Pentecost, He has exercised over the whole world through His mystical body the Church. The Church of God is the kingdom of Jesus Christ, a supernatural kingdom, resting indeed upon the basis of the natural world, but verifying our Lord's own words when He said, "My kingdom is not of this world. If My kingdom were of this world, My servants would certainly strive that I should not be delivered to the Jews: but now My kingdom is not from hence."* The fountain and source of His sovereignty is in the eternal order; and the operations, and powers, and prerogatives of His kingdom are supernatural. Our divine Lord, therefore, is invested with the fulness of all sovereign prerogatives, eternal and temporal, natural and supernatural. This, I think, no one will dispute who believes in Christianity.

But, secondly, our divine Lord communicated to His Church upon earth, and pre-eminently to His Vicar, the Head of the Church on earth, the chief of His twelve Apostles, a portion of His sovereignty. His eternal sovereignty He did not communicate. This no creature is capable of wielding. Nor even the whole of His temporal sovereignty did He communicate; for He has reserved to Himself exclusively the administration and government of His own providence. All that divine action of our Lord which is manifested in the operations of Providence, attaches to Him as God, and, although exercised in time,

* St. John xviii. 36.

belongs exclusively to His Person. But the spiritual and supernatural sovereignty of His kingdom He vested in His Church on earth, in His Apostles, and above all in him who was the chief of the Apostles. First of all, He established upon earth a jurisdiction which has a divine fountain, and that fountain is the Person of the incarnate Son of God, who said, " I dispose unto you a kingdom, as My Father hath disposed unto Me."* And again, " All power in heaven and earth is given unto Me," that is, the incarnate Son : "going therefore, teach ye all nations, baptizing them in the name of the Father, the Son, and Holy Ghost: teaching them to observe all things, whatsoever I have commanded you:" † thus imposing upon mankind a law of obedience. He gave the Apostles, therefore, a twofold jurisdiction: first, a jurisdiction over His sacramental and natural body, by virtue whereof they consecrated and constituted His eucharistic presence perpetually in His Church ; and secondly, a jurisdiction over His mystical body ; for when He breathed on them and said, " Receive ye the Holy Ghost; whose sins ye shall forgive, they are forgiven them, and whose sins you shall retain, they are retained;"‡ this is a jurisdiction over souls. And that gives us the interpretation of the words which He spoke to Peter: " I say to thee,

---

* St. Luke xxii. 29. † St. Matt. xxviii. 19, 20.
‡ St. John xx. 23.

That thou art Peter, and upon this rock I will build My Church, and the gates of hell shall not prevail against it. And I will give to thee the keys of the kingdom of heaven; and whatsoever thou shalt bind upon earth it shall be bound also in heaven, and whatsoever thou shalt loose on earth, it shall be loosed also in heaven." * In these words He gave to His Church a power, first to interpret and illustrate His law; then to execute and enforce the obligations of that law; and further, judicially to try the souls of men according to that law, and coercively to bind them to obedience to that law. He thereby constituted a real and proper sovereignty on earth, spiritual, supernatural, and He committed it to His Church.

Now, this second principle I conceive no one will dispute who believes in the institution of the visible Church. No Catholic can hesitate for an instant in professing his faith that these supernatural and spiritual prerogatives which were wielded by the Son of God in person, attach to His Vicar on earth.

III. Then, thirdly, this spiritual sovereignty of His Church entered into the Roman empire. It came, as it were, like a life from heaven, to animate the vast political organisation which God in His divine providence had already established in the world, Perhaps you will say, that then the Church was subject to the empire. It is exactly to this point that

* St. Matt. xvi. 18, 19.

St. Paul speaks when he says, "Let every soul be subject to the higher powers." It was at the very time when this Church of God entered into the Roman empire, that St. Paul met the conscience by declaring as the law of God, that every power is ordained of God, and that every soul should be subject to a higher power. Tertullian, writing in the second century, says, that the emperor was "a man only less than God Himself."* The early Christians obeyed the Roman emperors, and paid tribute. Perhaps it may seem as if these facts were contrary to the argument I am about to use. Not so; they form the very basis of the argument. For three hundred years, while the empire was heathen, the Church was what was called an unlawful society,† prohibited by

* Tertull. ad Scapulam, § 2 : "Colimus ergo et imperatorem sic, quomodo et nobis licet et ipsi expedit, ut hominem a Deo secundum : et quicquid est, a Deo consecutum et solo Deo minorem. Hoc et ipse volet : sic enim omnibus major est, dum solo vero Deo minor est."

† Analecta Juris Pontificii, livraison 35, ch. ii. : "Un édit de Jules-César, confirmé par les empereurs qui régnèrent après lui, avait pour objet de proscire d'une manière générale tout colláge ou toute communauté non-approuvé par le sénat et par les empereurs. Or, voici en peu de mots le parti que les légistes ont osé tirer de ce fameux édit. 1. Les églises ou les collèges chrétiens constituaient des compagnies des corps distincts du commun des citoyens, d'après ce principe du *Digeste* (liv. xlvii. tit. 22, de collegiis) : 'Sodales sunt qui ejusdem collegii sunt, quam Græci hæteriam vocant.' 2. Les étéries furent prohibées par Jules-César (voir Josephus, lib. xiv. Antiq.), puis par Trajan (v. Baronius ad ann. 100, n. 8 et 9), et enfin au nom de l'empire tout entier par Septime-Sévère qui fut

the laws of the empire. The laws of the empire forbade the existence of any society or corporation not recognised by its own legislation. Nevertheless, for three hundred years the Church of God existed, in virtue of its own spiritual sovereignty, in the face of the imperial laws. Again, it was forbidden by the laws of the empire that any society not recognised by those laws should hold property. Nevertheless, for three hundred years the Church continued to possess. The laws of the empire forbade any worship other than that of the recognised religions.* Nevertheless, for three hundred years the Christian worship existed, and that through the whole circumference of the Roman empire, and even in Rome itself. The Church, therefore, was on three points in direct

proclamé Auguste vers l'an 195 d'après la chronologie du Cardinal Baronius. D'où il résulte qu' aucune société ne pouvait être regardée comme licite, et devait au contraire être dissoute, si elle n'avait pas été autorisée à se constituer par autorité du sénat ou de l'empereur. Par conséquent durant les trois premiers siècles les colléges ou, en d'autres termes, les églises ou, réunions des chrétiens furent entièrement illicites, et par conséquent incapables d'acquérir des biens. Pour avoir la capacité d'acquérir des immeubles, il aurait fallu que ces réunions fussent déclarées vrais colléges et réunions légitimes par le pouvoir séculier, mais cela n'eut lieu que sous le règne de Constantin. 3. Durant les premiers siècles les chrétiens n'eurent en leur faveur à diverses reprises, qu'une simple tolérance, pour l'exercice privé de leur religion : sans que cela pût les rendre capables de posséder des biens comme société.

* Gosselin, Power of the Pope in the Middle Ages, vol. i. p. 22, and notes.

and diametrical disobedience to this sovereign power which was ordained of God. And why? Because the empire had exceeded its limits. The Church has a sovereignty of its own. The Christians paid tribute to the emperor, as our Lord paid tribute, "that we may not scandalise them." * They honoured this great principle of obedience to a power which *de facto* —that is, as a matter of providential fact—existed. For three hundred years, almost every Pontiff that ascended the throne of St. Peter sat on a throne steeped in blood. Submissively and patiently, "as sheep for the slaughter," † as the Apostle says in this same epistle, they gave themselves to die for the faith. They offered no active resistance to the laws of the empire; but they could not obey, and were resigned to suffer. For three hundred years, then, the Church had over it, in Rome itself, a temporal power, to which it rendered obedience in all things that were lawful. In this it only obeyed the precept, "Render unto Cæsar the things that are Cæsar's, and unto God the things that are God's." ‡

But from the hour when Constantine, in the language of the Roman law, § "Deo jubente," by the command of God, translated the seat of empire to Constantinople, from that moment there never reigned

---

* St. Matt. xvii. 26.   † Rom. viii. 36.   ‡ St. Luke xx. 25.
§ Dominicus Soto, De Potestate Ecclesiasticâ, — Bibliotheca Pontif. Roccaberti, tom. x. p. 136.

in Rome a temporal prince to whom the Bishops of Rome owed a permanent allegiance. From that hour God Himself liberated His Church.* It was from the first involved in the principles of the supernatural sovereignty of the Church on earth, that it should be one day free from all temporal allegiance, though as yet its liberation was not accomplished. David possessed the promise of the kingdom of Israel; but he waited long. Jeroboam had the promise of the ten tribes; but he was a usurper, because he grasped it before the time. The Church followed not the example of Jeroboam, but that of David, whose Son is its own divine Head. It waited until such time as God should break its bonds asunder, and should liberate it from subjection to civil powers, and enthrone it in the possession of a temporal sovereignty of its own.† Therefore, in that day when the first Christian emperor withdrew himself into the far East, he abandoned Rome and Italy; and the "donation" of Constantine, as it is called, expresses not a fact, but a principle. Constantine signed no instrument of donation; but the manner of conceiving and of speaking in those simple ages, so represented the providential

---

* Suarez, Opuscula, De Immunitate Ecclesiastica, lib. iv. 3: "Dicendum ergo est summum Pontificem ex divino jure habere exemptionem et immunitatem ab omni judicio ac jurisdictione sæculari etiam imperatorum et regum."

† The temporal power belongs to all Christians.

fact of the donation of God. God gave to the Vicar of His Son the possession of the city in which thirty of his predecessors had sealed their testimony with their blood. The donation of Constantine consisted in the simple providential fact, that he departed from Rome to Constantinople, moved by an impulse from God Himself. It would delay me too long to dwell upon the motives which God implanted in the first Christian emperor, to impel him to abandon his sovereignty in Rome. They were motives of a supernatural origin, and he was but obeying a supernatural impulse. The donation was of God, and not of man. Simple ages have supposed that the great act was engrossed upon a parchment, illuminated, sealed, and signed, and laid upon the altar of St. Peter. This, as a fable, represents most truly the act of Divine Providence. Now, perhaps in some histories you will be told that the Greek emperors used still to claim possession over Italy; that they sent their exarchs and their armies to Ravenna and to Rome. You will be told also, that afterwards the kings of France claimed it; that the French emperors, Pepin and Charlemagne, claimed Italy and Rome as their own. So the world writes history. Such is not the fact. Would any man maintain that Britain was part of the Roman empire when the Roman legions abandoned it, to be trodden down by hordes of pagans and steeped in its own blood? Does any man who reads the history of Britain maintain that Britain was a province of the empire of Constantinople? From the moment when the last Roman legion withdrew its foot from the shores of Britain, it was liberated by the providence of God, and possessed an independence of its own. From that day spring up the first blades of the Anglo-Saxon kingdoms, the English monarchy, and the empire of Great Britain. Just as the liberated and independent sovereignty of Britain is related to the withdrawal of the last Roman legion that left its shores, so the independence of Italy and Rome dates from the moment when the emperors of the East abandoned it. From that time there never was a moment when the emperors of the East could so much as protect Rome. Italy and Rome were given over providentially to the purgation of fire and of blood. A sea of blood mingled with fire descended from the steeps of the Alps when Goths, Vandals, Visigoths, Huns, and Lombards in successive generations poured over the plains of Italy. Rome itself was saved again and again only by the fortitude of the Roman Pontiffs, by a Divine presence, and by supernatural protection, which turned back the barbarian chiefs Attila and Genseric and others when within the very sight of its walls.

Again, when Pepin descended into Italy to deliver the exarchate of Ravenna, the capital of that very Romagna which is now the centre of discord;

when he drove out the Lombards who had usurped the patrimony of the Church, we are told that he again made a donation to the Church. Not so; the very word in his act was this, that he made "restitution to the Church and to the (Roman) republic."*—that is, the commonwealth of the people and city of Rome—of that portion of territory which had been usurped from them by the Lombards. Again, when Charlemagne once more delivered Ravenna, and even Rome itself, he at the same time declared that he made a restitution, not a donation.†

---

* Anastasius, Vita S. Stephani II. Papæ, p. 1623. "Porrò christianissimus Pippinus Francorum rex, ut vere beati Petri fidelis [*i.e.* defensor] atque jam tanti sanctissimi pontificis salutiferis obtemperans monitis, direxit suos missos Aistulpho nequissimo Longobardorum regi, propter pacis fœdera, et præfatæ sanctæ Dei *Ecclesiæ ac reipublicæ restituenda jura:* atque bis et tertio eum deprecatus est, et plura ei pollicitus est munera, ut tantummodo pacificè propria *restitueret* propriis" . . . p. 1626. "Spopondit ipse Aistulphus cum universis suis judicibus [*i.e.* magnatibus] sub terribili et fortissimo sacramento, atque in eodem pacti fœdere per scriptam paginam affirmavit, se illicò *redditurum* civitatem Ravennatium cum aliis diversis civitatibus." Labbe, Concil. viii. Epist. v. Stephani Papæ II. ad Francos : "Sin autem quod non credimus et aliquam posueritis moram aut adinventionem minime velociter hanc nostram adimplendam adhortationem, ad liberandam hanc *meam civitatem Romanam* et populum in ea commorantem, sanctam Dei apostolicam ecclesiam a Domino mihi commissam simul et ejus præsulem : sciatis vos ex auctoritate sanctæ et unicæ Trinitatis per gratiam Apostolatus quæ data est mihi a Christo Domino vos alienari pro transgressione nostræ adhortationis a regno Dei et vita æterna."

† Anastasius, Vita Adriani I. p. 1735. " Ipsi Francorum missi,

Though included nominally for a time, Central Italy and Rome were providentially and in fact eliminated and excluded from all civil dominion; from the moment the empire was translated, they have stood out from the circle of all other sovereignties, resting on a sovereignty of their own; and neither the empire of the Franks, nor the empire of the Germans, much less the empire of the Greeks, has ever included Rome within its circumference from that hour.

I say, then, that it was God's own act which liberated His Vicar upon earth from subjection to temporal power; and that for twelve hundred years the Bishops of Rome have reigned as temporal princes. They have possessed their own. No man has given to them their sovereign rights. They reign there as Christian princes by the providence of God. They are the first example of a Christian monarchy, the first seed of Christian Europe, the first roll of Christian sovereigns. When France was yet distracted by con-

properantes cum apostolicæ sedis missis, declinaverunt ad Desiderium: qui et constanter eum deprecantes adhortati sunt, sicut illis a suo rege præceptum exstitit, ut antefatas, quas abstulerat civitates, pacifice beato Petro *redderet*, et justitias parti Romanorum faceret: sed minime quidquam horum apud eum obtinere valuerunt, asserentem se minime quidquam *redditurum* . . . . sed dum in tanta duritia protervus ipse permaneret rex Desiderius, cupiens antedictus christianissimus Francorum rex pacifice justitias beati Petri recipere, direxit eidem Longobardorum regi, ut solummodo tres obsides Longobardorum judicum filios illi tradidisset, pro *istis restituendis civitatibus.*"

flicting races, when England was divided by the Heptarchy, when Germany was a forest, and when Spain was a desolation, the Vicar of Christ already reigned as a sovereign prince in Rome.

IV. Another principle, then, which I affirm is this: that God, who providentially liberated the Vicar of His Son from subjection to any civil power, did by the same Divine Providence bestow on him the right to what he holds. In order to make clear what I mean, let me call your attention more particularly to three points. The first is this: that the possession of the patrimony, as it is called, of the Church, is by Divine right on the part of him who receives it; secondly, on the part of Him who gives it; and thirdly, on the part of him who holds it. If there be any property sacred upon earth,—if there be any property on earth which is constituted by Divine Providence,—it is the patrimony of the Church, on the part of him that receives, on the part of Him that gives, and on the part of him that possesses.

I have said already, that during the three hundred years while it was forbidden by the imperial laws that any society should hold property except such corporations as were recognised by those laws, the Church, as a society and as a corporation, did hold houses, lands, and goods.* And why? Because the Church of God is not a society put together by a human legis-

* Analecta Juris Pontificii, lib. xxxv. c. 2.

lature. It is not a corporation of voluntary individuals, who unite themselves by their free will, to dissolve themselves to-morrow. It is a society of divine origin, and a corporation of a supernatural institution. It has its being, its unity, its construction, and all its properties, from a power which is divine. Therefore, as a society of divine institution, it is possessed of rights higher in kind than any human society; and among those rights it has the right of holding property. They who in the beginning believed, sold their houses and lands, and laid the price at the Apostles' feet.* And the price which was laid at their feet the Apostles held as their own by a divine right. No man could have taken it away without sacrilege. So, in after ages, lands and houses (which became the first Christian churches) were given to the Church throughout the whole of the Roman empire. The church of St. Pudentiana was the house of St. Pudens, a Roman senator. So again the church of St. Clement, the church of St. Caius, and numberless others in Rome, were once the houses of patricians. House and land, site and dwelling-place, were given to the Christians, and thereby became the possessions of the Church. And the Church held these things by divine right; though the laws of the empire forbade it to possess. It was not a society allowed by the law, but it held by a higher title.

* Acts iv. 34, 35.

And this right of possession in the Church is inherent and inalienable to this day.

Next, there is a right on the part of Him that gives. Every man has a right to dispose of that which he possesses. The dictum of the lawyers of this world, that property is the creation of the state, is not true. Property is not the creation of civil law; it is the creation of God in nature and in providence. The true creator and maker of property is God, not man, and He has constituted His Church with a right of receiving gifts in His name. The civil powers and the civil law of the world have the right of disposal over that which is their own. But the principle of property lies deeper. What the Church holds, it holds in its own right, as it did in the three hundred years when all the imperial laws were against it. Though the current of imperial laws may have run in later ages in its favour, it is not the imperial legislation which gives to the Church the right to possess what is its own. It holds it of itself, by the providence of God, of its own inherent right. The Church, therefore, possesses its patrimony by a more perfect right than that of any crowned prince to the territory over which he reigns. In the time of St. Gregory the Great, the Church possessed many patrimonies.* We hear, at this day, only of the patrimony of St. Peter. But the Church called all its possessions patrimonies.

* S. Gregorii Vita, auct. Joan. Diacono, lib. ii. c. 53-55 seq.

There was also the patrimony of St. Apollinaris, at Ravenna; and the patrimony of St. Ambrose, at Milan. The patrimonies of the Church of Rome were twenty-three in number. They were in Calabria, in Sicily, in Africa, in Sardinia, in Corsica, in Gaul, in Piedmont, and in Lombardy, besides that which is now called the patrimony of St. Peter. And all these the Church possessed by a right higher than the will of man.

Now, that which the Church possesses as its own, the Church may give, but no man may take away. The Church has power and dominion over its own possessions, to hold them, or to give them; for the essence of property is enjoyment and power of disposition. As in times of famine and pestilence at Milan St. Charles took the chalices from the altar, broke them, and gave them among the poor for medicine and for food; so in like manner the Church might at this day do as it has done before—give its patrimony. But no man may take a chalice from the altar; and the man that takes it commits a sacrilege. The Pontiffs have in all ages declared, that he who lays hands by himself or by his officers on anything consecrated to the Church commits a sacrilege. The bulls of Popes and the Council of Trent* both launch against the man who lays his hand upon the possessions of the Church the sentence of excommunication.

* Concil. Trid. sess. xxv. c. 20.

And now, as to the third point, namely, that the line of Pontiffs hold to this day, by a right higher than of human creation, the patrimony of the Church, I need say no more. This principle is contained in the two already proved: and the possession of its patrimony is held at this hour by a divine right, fenced about by the sacred sanctions of the Church in its most express forms of legislation and of censure.

As God, by direct and divine providence, has bestowed possessions on the Vicar of His Son, so He has also bestowed temporal power. And this temporal power of the Holy See has, in a great measure, arisen from the possession of extensive patrimonies. If time permitted me, I would fain enter into one of the most beautiful chapters of Christian history. First of all, this patrimony was constituted of twenty-three* distinct portions, scattered all round Rome as its centre, the nucleus and beginning of Christian Europe. Of that I hope to speak hereafter. On these estates, each of which was called a Massa, the Church placed its own colonists. It was the first to send from Rome Christians into Pagan lands, civilised men into barbarous lands; and these civilised and Christian men introduced the first seeds of the Christian civil order. Wheresoever these Christian and civilised colonists went, emancipation from slavery followed. I can give only one or two instances. There are two beau-

* Analecta Juris Pontificii, lib. xxxv. c. 3.

tiful letters of St. Gregory addressed to the guardians of two of the patrimonies—one in Africa, and one elsewhere. In the first he begins by saying: "Our Lord and God Jesus Christ, having been incarnate for us, made Himself a servant, that we, through His servitude, might be made free. It is not meet, therefore, that man should hold his brother in service; and I therefore hereby remit and give their freedom to Montana and Thomas, two Christian slaves. To Montana, whom I know to desire to be entered as a religious into a monastery, I give also a sum of gold left to her by Gaudiosus, a presbyter, with my free permission that she shall go into the monastery of Constantina. To Thomas I give also a sum of money left by the same presbyter, but he will remain among the order of notaries"—that is, in the civil service of the Roman See. The other example is still more beautiful. There was a poor slave named Catella. Catella is one of the common servile names in the Latin tongue; and this poor Catella, as St. Gregory says in his letter, with prayers and tears had besought her master to give her her freedom, that she might become a nun. This was about A.D. 590. St. Gregory hearing of it, directs the guardians of the patrimony to go and buy Catella, and pay to her master the ransom of her freedom; then to give her liberty, that she might enter into the religious life.*

* Analecta Juris Pontificii, lib. xxxv. c. 6.

Those two instances are taken out of a vast harvest of acts of supernatural love and charity, whereby the action of the Church on its patrimonies laid the foundations of Christian Europe. It was in works of mercy like these that the political and executive power of the Church arose.*

Where, I would ask, is there a power in the world that holds its sovereignty by such titles as the Vicar of Christ? He holds it, as I have shown you, by the direct donation of Divine Providence. He holds it next by a willing conquest over loving hearts emancipated from slavery, and from a worse bondage than that of the body—from the slavery of sin and death. He holds it by the very choice of those people who fled to him when they had no other protector.† He holds it by a possession which is now fifteen hundred years old. He holds it by every right known in divine and human law. He held it before there was a Christian prince in Europe. We venerate the British empire as one of which the sovereign has a right to the obedience of her subjects. We render it gladly, and we lift no hand against that sovereignty—no, nor speak a word, nor conceive a seditious thought. Yet why? What right has she, who reigns so worthily over us, to the sovereign crown she wears, but that very same right which I claim for him who possesses

---

* Civiltà Cattolica, serie iv. vol. x. p. 67.
† Ibid. p. 66.

the temporal power of the Roman state? And not so much; for he was a prince when her sovereignty was unknown. She has received her sovereignty by the indirect providence of God; and he more. There is no right that can be found in human or divine law investing our sovereign with the sacred character to which we render our obedience, which is not to be found in greater fulness and in greater explicitness in the Vicar of Jesus Christ.

Now, I might dwell longer upon this. We find persons who are supposed to read history, ask, Where was the temporal sovereignty of the Popes in the first three hundred years? I would answer by asking them, Where was the British monarchy for eight hundred years? Perhaps they will say: But if it was of divine institution, why was it not instituted from the first? I should say, in answer: Ask the mysterious will of God. I might further ask: Why was it four thousand years before he sent His Son into the world, born of a woman? Why was it a long three hundred years before He gave to His people Israel a king, and established a monarchy over them? "It is not for you to know the times or moments, which the Father hath put in His own power;"* it is enough to know when God acts. When God has revealed His will in divine providence, it is enough; what He has accomplished is a power ordained of God.

* Acts i. 7.

V. And now, to make an end. We say that this power of the Popes is ordained of God. And it is ordained for reasons which are so explicit that I cannot pass them by, and yet cannot now dwell upon them. I will, however, touch them, because it is at this moment the fashion with some persons to use a language of mockery, to address the Vicar of Jesus Christ as they who in the Prætorium said, "Hail, King of the Jews!" When they hear it said, that the temporal power is necessary to the spiritual, they claim it as a concession; as if the spiritual power must be propped up by temporal power. And then we are told that St. Peter had no temporal sovereignty: and legislatures laugh, as if some great sally of genius, or some vast success of satirical wit, had for ever overthrown the temporal sovereignty of the Vicar of Jesus Christ. Of the reasons why God has so ordained it, two are plainly manifest. The first is, that the temporal power is the shelter of the spiritual. It may be compared to what is often seen in Italy—a beautiful canopy wrought out of stone over a pure well. It preserves it from the intermingling of any thing earthly; and the pure fountains break forth in all their brightness under this canopy of fretted architecture. The canopy is the work of the hand of man; but the fountain is the work of the will of God. Now, this temporal sovereignty, which has arisen in the direct providence of God, serves a like office.

It is in order that the Church shall in *perfect freedom* exercise its spiritual powers. I lay emphasis on the words, "perfect freedom." I do not say, it is that the Church may exercise its spiritual powers. For three hundred years it did so in the heart of a heathen empire. It did so through three hundred years of martyrdom—through ten persecutions, which were only ten special outbreaks of a persecution which was always in activity. It is not necessary to the Church to have a temporal power that it may exercise its spiritual power. St. Gregory VII. exercised his spiritual powers when he was at Salerno; Pius VII., when he was at Savona; Pius IX., when he was at Gaeta. But the alternative is this: the catacombs or the Vatican; martyrdom or sovereignty; warfare and persecution, or civil sovereignty and its relation to Christian monarchies and to Christian Europe. Choose which you will. The temporal power of the Pope is an integral part of that civil and Christian order through which the Church exercises in tranquillity and safety its spiritual office over the hearts of men, willing in their obedience. Destroy that temporal power, and the power of the Church will not be dissolved; but as in the beginning, so now, through seas of blood and waves of fire, will it have to wade its way in plucking souls from the burning. The work will be done, for it is the work of God; but it will be done so as by fire. When, therefore, it is said that the temporal power is necessary to the spiritual, what is meant is this,—it is necessary to the free and peaceful exercise of it.*

And a further reason is this: it is necessary to the fulfilment of the civil mission, and to the civilising action of the Church in the world, that it should be clothed with temporal power. This, however, is a subject we shall consider hereafter.

I will now only very briefly point to certain other reasons. The Church, being sovereign at its centre, is sovereign also in all its localities; wheresoever the Church of God is found throughout the world, the whole sovereignty of the Church is in that portion. It is, we know, the pride of the British subject, that he goes into the four quarters of the world, carrying with him the inherent rights of the British empire; and any man who lays a hand upon a British subject, wages war against the whole British empire. So in like manner the whole sovereignty of the Church of God is in every portion and every locality. And the poor scattered Church in England, made up of units in a vast population, has in it this sovereignty, because it rests upon the Holy See, and upon the twofold sovereignty of Jesus Christ. And lastly, and this point I can but state in a single word, the temporal sovereignty of the Holy See is the perpetual testi-

* Allocution of the Holy Father Pius IX., in Secret Consistory, May 20, 1851.

mony and witness against nationalism. Our divine Lord, when He redeemed mankind, extinguished all national distinctions. In Christ Jesus "there is neither Gentile nor Jew, circumcision nor uncircumcision, barbarian nor Scythian, bond nor free."[*] He put His royal foot, pierced on Calvary, on the nationalities of the world; and from that hour, nationalism in religion became schism. The principle of nationalism in the matter of religion is schism, and in politics revolution.

Now, it remains for me to draw only one conclusion: "let every soul be subject to higher powers; the powers that be are ordained of God. He that resisteth the power, resisteth the ordinance of God." Any man that lifts a hand, and that not merely an armed one, but an unarmed hand, against the temporal sovereignty of the Holy See, not only he that levies legions, but he who by thought, word, or deed, helps on the dissolution of the temporal sovereignty of the Pope, resists the ordinance of God. He that sows in the hearts of others seeds of disloyalty towards the Vicar of our divine Lord, that man is resisting the ordinance of God. Any man who in his mind conceives thoughts of disaffection, or of contempt; who with approval reads that which is every day poured out like an inundation in this country, scorn and hatred and satire against the old man that reigns in

[*] Col. iii. 11.

the Vatican; any man that takes into his heart those disloyal and unfilial thoughts,—that man is resisting the ordinance of God. The providential state in which the Vicar of Jesus Christ is manifested upon earth, is the work of God Himself; and he who in this, by thought, word, or deed resists him, resists the ordinance of God. We owe to him fidelity, loyalty, and love; not only do we owe to him obedience, we owe to him an interior fidelity, the loyalty of our hearts.

LECTURE II.

I NOW proceed, in pursuance of the plan I have laid down, to justify, so far as my limited opportunity allows, what you may consider the strong assertions made in the first Lecture.

Those assertions were as follows: that the temporal power of the Pope is ordained of God; next, that it is the productive and sustaining cause of Christian Europe; and thirdly, that its dissolution would be the dissolution of Christian Europe. From which propositions I deduced these conclusions: first, that he who resists it, resists a power ordained of God; secondly, that he who lends a hand or a tongue to its dissolution, does, so far as co-operation extends, help to the dissolution of Christian Europe; and that all who directly or indirectly contribute to that result, will, according to their proportion, purchase to themselves judgment.

Now, before I take up this subject, I desire, in the words of St. Peter to the people of Jerusalem, to say, first to any among you who may not be of the unity of the Church, but of the people of this great nation, whose hostility to the temporal power of the Pope is a tradition in their history, "I know, brethren, that you did it through ignorance, as also did your rulers."* I wish at once to declare, that I hope multitudes may be innocent of the opposition which by word and deed they are thus offering to the temporal power of the Holy See; because I believe that being born and nurtured in a profound ignorance of the principles of the Church, and of the history of Christian Europe, they know not what they do. Secondly, there may be among you those who are of the unity of the Catholic Church, but, having been born under the shadows of peaceful times, have never been compelled to analyse or to study the first principles of this subject, and therefore are drawn—some, it may be, by political opinions which they have inherited, or by strong patriotic sentiments which may be a second nature to them—if not into opposition, at least into a state of doubt upon this great subject. I wish to say also, that I believe their state of hesitation, and even their present disposition to take the wrong side, comes not from a perverseness of the will, but from an indistinctness of the intellect; this I wish to say from the outset; because, though it has been my duty in the years past often to say the strongest things in the strongest language,—and such I believe to be the duty of a priest of God in the world, never to flinch, or to

---

* Acts iii. 17.

explain away the message committed to him,—I have ever desired to avoid the evils of controversy, or in any way to tinge or to embitter the words I use with anything of animosity or of personal feeling.

Now, before I begin the subject of to-day, which is, that the temporal power of the Popes has been the productive and sustaining principle of Christian Europe, I wish to recall to you the results of the former Lecture. I have set before you the first great principle of the sovereignty, temporal and eternal, spiritual—that is supernatural—and natural, of our divine Lord Jesus Christ, who is not only "the great High Priest," but "the King of kings, and Lord of lords." I set also before you another great principle, namely, that our divine Lord committed to His Church, and to his Vicar, the Head on earth of that Church, His spiritual sovereignty, reserving to Himself His temporal or providential sovereignty; and that, therefore, the spiritual sovereignty of the Church is a divine institution, and has a power directly ordained of God. Thirdly, that there are other powers in the world which are indirectly ordained of God; namely, all temporal sovereignties. Further, I showed you that St. Paul declares that even the heathen empire of Rome, and the power of a heathen emperor, Nero, the greatest persecutor of the Church, was ordained of God; and as such, had a claim to submission and obedience. I then showed you how, by an indirect but divine providence, our divine Lord has liberated His Vicar on earth, in the plenitude of his spiritual sovereignty, from all civil subjection; first by the translation to the East, and then by the eventual extinction of the Roman empire in Italy. I showed, fourthly, how by the same providence, indirect indeed, but nevertheless divine, our Lord clothed His Vicar with the possession of a patrimony, which was as distinctly a donation from God as if he had received it from His visible hand. And I showed, lastly, that upon the basis of this temporal possession our divine Lord has raised a temporal power by His indirect operation—and that therefore the temporal power of the Popes is a divine ordinance, having divine sanction, at least, equally with every other sovereignty in the world. Therefore, all that can be claimed for our own sovereign, can be claimed equally for the Supreme Pontiff; and more than this, in so far as the divine sanction of the temporal power is higher, in proportion as the person who is clothed with it is a more special subject of the Divine providence, and has a character and a capacity of receiving sovereignty and of exercising a supreme direction in the affairs of men higher and greater than all the princes of the world.

And from this, you will remember, I deduced two conclusions; first, that the temporal power is providentially ordained for the free exercise of the spiritual. And I there drew a further distinction, which I beg you to bear in mind. It has been asked, Where was the temporal power of the Popes in the time of St. Peter? If it is necessary to the spiritual now, why was it not necessary then? To which I answered, It is not necessary to the spiritual office of the Church. The Church can exercise its spiritual office in martyrdom, and has done it. For three hundred years it wrestled with the world, and subdued it, though under the sword of the executioner. The spiritual office of the Apostles is perpetual and independent, because divine. It owes nothing to temporal power. But I said that the temporal power of the Popes is necessary to the peaceful and tranquil exercise of the spiritual power; and that the alternative is this, whether the spiritual power of the Church shall be exercised through martyrdom and persecution, or in peace and in harmony with the civil order of the world. They who desire the dissolution of the temporal power, not knowing what they do, would reduce the world to barbarism, and the Church to a condition of persecution. The Church would, notwithstanding, still exercise its spiritual sovereignty and its spiritual office with the same divine efficacy and power, but through persecution, not in peace.

Having thus disposed of the first part of the subject, the next point in order is this: that the temporal power of the Pope is necessary to the civil mission of the Church in the world; that, in the discharge of this civil mission, the temporal power of the Holy See has been the principle, first of the production, and then of the maintenance, of Christian Europe; that the civil order of Christendom is the offspring of the temporal power with which our divine Lord providentially clothed His Vicar upon earth. The time is indeed short for such a subject, and therefore all I can do is this : to state to you the great principles in outline, and ask you to believe that I will not state any fact which I have not verified, or which I am not prepared to maintain by historical proofs.

I. The first principle with which I begin is this, that the Son of God became incarnate for us. If any man disbelieve this, I cannot argue with him about the Vicar of Jesus Christ. If he believe this, he believes that our Lord came into the world to take our manhood, first to unite it to the Godhead in His own Person, and then to make it the instrument of the elevation, the sanctification, and the perfection of the human race;—that when He came into the world, He chose to Himself certain disciples, who, by converse with Himself, by the illumination of His divine mind, and by the charity of His sacred heart, were changed, transformed, and assimilated to His own likeness;— that He then united them into one fellowship, that He bestowed upon them a supernatural unity, and thereby created a visible society united to His Person, and united within itself;—and that He bestowed an organisation upon that living body of which He was Himself the Head, and, as I have said, the productive and sustaining principle. I say, further, that He opened a fountain of jurisdiction within this society, and appointed it to be in the world as the leaven in the meal, the regenerating principle of mankind; to be to the world what the soul is to the body, that which informs it, guides it, directs it, which even impresses upon the features a certain countenance and character.

II. I say, secondly, that the Catholic Church, which springs from the Incarnation, discharges in the world the same functions in regard to the nations of the world as our divine Lord in regard to His disciples. It has a twofold mission: first to convert and to save individuals, one by one, as by the apostolic missions; and next, having converted individuals and families, cities and nations, to assimilate, to change, to transform, to unite, to organise them like as our divine Lord did with His disciples. And this it has effected by the knowledge of the Word of God, which the world had not before; by the perfect law of right and wrong, that is, the divine law of justice; then by the perfection of its own constitution, by its monarchical form, by the spirit of liberty and freedom among all its members, by the unity of its jurisdiction from which all authority has issued, and by the world-wide organisation which binds the nations of the world into one family, according to the command of our Lord, "Going therefore, teach ye all nations, baptizing them in the name of the Father, Son, and Holy Ghost." And thus has arisen Christendom, the great Christian family spread throughout the world. What, then, was its productive cause and root? The Incarnation, and the visible Church which springs from it. What is the trunk which supports Christendom to this day but that same visible Church, around which it was woven and entwined? What, then, was the seed and stem of Christendom but the Holy See, the centre of that Church, the source of the spiritual powers which have taken to themselves and assimilated the civil powers of the world. This, then, is the general principle I desire now to dwell on.

III. When the Church went out into the world, it found there a vast empire, which covered it with a perfect organisation, social and political. It had one chief city reigning over the whole world; it had one emperor, whose will was the fountain of all law; one senate, one legislature, one code of laws. It had one political organisation uniting all nations, and one vast military system holding all people in subjection. It had one great chart, and one centre, the *milliarium aureum*, the golden mile-stone which stood by the arch of Severus, upon which were marked all the distances throughout the world-wide empire of Rome. It was ruled by the most perfect and minute legislation which had ever governed the natural order of the world.

Perhaps you may think that it was this organisation which the Church took possession of. No; before the Church assumed its civil mission to create modern Europe, the seven vials from heaven were poured out upon that empire, and the seven trumpets blew, and the four winds of heaven were let loose, and the great angel cast the mighty stone into the sea, and said, "Babylon the great is fallen;" for that great empire was ravaged, desolated, and pillaged by the invasion of barbarians, by hordes from every quarter, until there remained of all its structures scarcely anything but mutilated ruins of its greatness, its aqueducts, its military roads, the Flavian amphitheatre, and the Pantheon. Before Almighty God sent His Church out into the world on its civil mission, the whole of that vast empire was burnt up as by fire and deluged by blood. Italy became a desolation, and Africa was abandoned to itself, and Britain was cast off, and Spain was forgotten; for the empire departed to Constantinople: the Byzantine emperors were feeble and helpless; they were harassed by the assaults of the Oriental tribes, and Italy they were no longer able even to protect. This is what all historians tell us. There was a time when even Rome itself is said to have been without a living inhabitant, when foxes ran over the Palatine Hill, and their bark alone was heard in the golden house of the Cæsars. Such was Rome, this mighty Rome, which once had some two millions of inhabitants, and twelve miles of diameter stretching from the Mediterranean Sea to the Sabine Hills—it was gone to desolation. And for centuries after this, it was ever and again the object of attack. It was besieged, it was sacked, it was ruined again and again. All its civil power had departed; and its sovereignty existed no more.

IV. It was into such a world as this that the Church was sent forth to do its work. Christian Europe is not the remains of the old Roman empire— it is a new creation. Small portions of that empire, which were cast off, took root and sprang into new life; but the structure of Christendom as a whole is entirely a new world, and has been the creation of Christianity. This, however, is a subject upon which it is impossible for me further to dwell. I must refer you to books; and if you desire to find an unprejudiced and impartial witness for my cause, take such a history as that of the infidel historian Gibbon. The book indeed is one which I commend to nobody, for nothing more mischievous or more poisonous can be found; yet nevertheless out of his own mouth is the acknowledgment to be taken. It is true that for some three hundred years after the empire was translated to Constantinople, the Bishops of Rome continued nominally under the empire of the East; just as David, during the long years he waited for the kingdom of Israel, was under the sovereignty of Saul, though the rightful king, the future heir, and already, I may say, invested with kingship. Though pursued and fugitive, he never lifted a hand to possess himself of that which God had promised him. So during those three hundred years secular writers may find, and make much of, instances in which the Bishops of Rome published the decrees of the emperors of the East, in the same way as David submitted to Saul. But during those three hundred years the emperors of the East not only could never effectually protect Italy, they never could so much as drive out the Huns, or the Vandals, or the Goths, or the Heruli, or any of the hordes of invaders. Except during some ten years of transitory triumph, soon to be dissipated, these hordes unceasingly harassed and afflicted Italy. Far from defending Rome, the heretical and schismatical spirit of Constantinople, throughout the whole of Italy, divided and embroiled its civil peace. It was only through the fidelity and firmness of several of the Pontiffs that the people of Italy were restrained from open rebellion against the emperors of Constantinople. Then again, when the Lombards had possessed themselves of Northern Italy, one of their most powerful kings took possession of Ravenna and Bologna, the exarchate or patrimony which is now in question. The reigning Pope, Stephen II., called in the help of a king of France, which, during the fifth and sixth centuries, had sprung up into a monarchy. The letter by which he was invited is commonly quoted and ridiculed for an expression which is so explicit to our purpose that it seems as if it was providentially used. The Pope writes: "I, Peter, call upon you, my sons, to protect my city of Rome." And the king of France, having crossed the Alps and vanquished the Lombards, " restored," as his word is, the exarchate of Ravenna, the Romagna included, to the Bishop of Rome and to the Roman commonwealth.* Having restored it, he was created a patrician of Rome; that is, he received the highest civil dignity under the sovereign of Rome, and he received it from the hand of the Bishop of Rome. It did not make him lord of Rome, nor prince of Rome, nor did it involve civil subjection on the part of Rome or of its Bishop. He was but the champion, as he was the son; he was the protector of the Holy See, and nothing more. It was a civil creation; the first civil office conferred in Rome for the protection of Rome, was a creation of the Pontiff. From whom, then, came this power but from him, whom our Lord had already clothed with the temporal possession, and therefore with the temporal power, of the abandoned city of Rome? In like manner, when Charlemagne again delivered the same province, and again restored it

---

* Supra, p. 15 and note.

he also in the same words was declared a Roman patrician. Later, he was consecrated emperor; but the empire gave him no right whatever over Rome as its sovereign. He was still no more than protector, champion, guardian of the Holy See. Rome was external to the empire of Charlemagne, as it was external to the empire of Constantinople; it had been abandoned and cast off in the providential order, and it had risen up into a sovereignty of its own.

At that time, I ask you, what was Spain? what was Germany? what was England? what was Europe? They were marshes and forests, and their people were moving hordes, in a state of internecine war one with another. The civil order of Europe, which diplomatists consider to be a creation of their own, had no existence. In those times of the fabulous history of most states of modern Europe, the Vicar of Jesus Christ was already reigning in Rome, and had created patricians to protect his civil peace. To put an illustration of the action of the Catholic Church upon Europe at large, I take the example of Spain and of England. Spain, I may say, has been created by the eighteen councils of Toledo; it was a Gothic and heretical nation; it was invaded by Moors; one-half of it was in the power of the Mahometans; it was infected by Judaism; it was subdivided into conflicting kingdoms. Then by the long line of the councils of Toledo, in which the Bishops of the Church of Spain sat with the princes and rulers of the land in united council, Spain was organised, consolidated, and raised into a sole monarchy. Take, again, the case of England; go back and read the history of the heptarchy, and of the Anglo-Saxon Church after the union of the seven kingdoms into one. Read, for instance, such works as Johnsons' *Canons* or Spelman's *Councils*, or the greater work of Wilkins; or, if you will, take a much more familiar book, Palgrave's *History of the English Commonwealth;* and you will find that the whole of England was organised by the united action of the spiritual and civil powers sitting in councils, which councils had a twofold character, ecclesiastical and civil, united in one. Indeed, as the writers of that day remark, it is difficult to say whether they were parliaments, or whether they were synods. So in the assizes throughout the country the Bishop and the Earl sat, side by side, delivering justice. In truth, our whole civil system has grown up from the creative power of the Church, operating on those rude ages, until it arose to the maturity in which we see it now.

Now what we see in regard to Spain and England is precisely what the Catholic and Roman Church has effected throughout the whole world. The German empire in the seventh and eighth centuries, then Hungary, France, and the lesser states of Europe, have slowly risen under its creative power. But who, I ask, has been the leader, the guide, and the legislator of this Christian Europe—who but the Supreme Pontiff? What Bishop of any of the other Sees can be put in comparison with any single Pontiff, though he be the least powerful and illuminated in that long line, in the action and work of creating Christian Europe? And the kingdoms, which, in the first instance, rose up under the power and influence of the Holy See, were consecrated, concentrated, and united into one great confederacy, were held together by a general law, by a transcendent principle of community, which operated through them all, and bound them all to one centre, and gave them all one arbitrator. Read the history of St. Gregory VII., or the history of Innocent III., and you will see that I have understated the truth, when I say that it was the special and personal action of the Pontiffs which created Christian Europe.

V. Now the last point on which I will dwell is this: that as the Church of God has created—and that specially through the action of the Supreme Pontiffs in their civil mission to the world—this vast and fair fabric of Christian Europe, so it has perpetually sustained it. I ask, what has given it coherence? What is it that has kept alive the governing principle among men, but that pure faith or knowledge of God which has gone forth from the Holy See, and has filled the whole circumference of Christendom? What has bound men together in the respect due to mutual rights, but that pure morality which was delivered to the Church as Guardian, and of which the Holy See is the supreme interpreter? These two streams, which, as St. Cyprian says in his treatise on the unity of the Church, are like the rays that flow from the sun, or like the streams that rise and break from the fountains, illuminated and inundated the whole Christian world. Now, I ask, what has preserved this in security, but the infallibility of the Church of God, vested chiefly and finally in the person of the Vicar of Jesus Christ? It will rather belong to the next Lecture to note how, by contrast, this may be proved, and how those nations which have separated themselves from the unity of the Catholic Church, and therefore are in opposition to the temporal sovereignty of Rome, have lost these two great principles of their preservation. I ask, then, what has preserved Christian Europe, but the principle of obedience, the precept of submission, which has been taught throughout the whole of its circuit by the Church of God, especially through the mouths of its Pontiffs? By them, subjects have been taught obedience, and rulers have learned justice. What, I ask, has limited monarchy? what has made monarchy a free institution, and supreme power compatible with the personal liberty of the people, but the limitations which the Holy See, acting through its Pontiffs, has imposed upon the princes of the world? Does anybody doubt these two propositions? To them I would say, the Pontiffs, with their temporal power, have been accused of despotism, at least, then, let us give them the credit of having taught the people to submit. They have been also accused of tyranny over princes; at least, let us give them the honour of having taught kings that their power is limited. The dread chimera at which the English people especially stand in awe, the deposing power of the Pope,—what was it but that supreme arbitration whereby the highest power in the world, the Vicar of the incarnate Son of God, anointed high priest, and supreme temporal ruler, sat in his tribunal, impartially to judge between nation and nation, between people and prince, between sovereign and subject? The deposing power grew up by the providential action of God, teaching to subjects obedience, and to princes clemency.

Now in this twofold power of the Popes, which has been, I may say, the centre of the diplomacy of Christian Europe, we see the sacerdotal and royal powers vested in one person, the two powers of king and priest, which are the two conservative principles of the Christian world. All Christian kings and all Christian priests stand related to the one person who bears in fulness that twofold character; and it is by adherence to that one person, as the centre of the civil and spiritual system, which grew up under his hand, that Christian Europe is preserved. I would say further, that, vast and solid as Christendom may seem, like a vault of stone,—the temporal power of the Pope is the keystone. Strike it out, and the family of nations would at once fall in ruins.

I will conclude now with two remarks: the first is this, that the history of civilisation is the history of Christianity. The civilisation of the natural order, before Christianity came into the world, has perished like Ninive under the sands of the desert; in itself it was corrupt and godless: true civilisation dates from the Incarnation. We count our Christian order *anno Domini*. It is based upon the Incarnation and upon Christianity; and the Vicar of the incarnate Son of God has been the head and leader of the civilisation of Europe. Now the history of Christianity is the history of the Christian Church. Will you go to Oriental sects, to the Gnostics, for instance, or to some of the almost nameless and forgotten forms of perverted Christianity, to ascertain what Christianity is? Will you even go to the Greek schism, the China of Christendom for exclusiveness and stagnation? Will you go to those nations of the West, which, by their separation from the Church, have filled the whole world with a tumult of conflicting societies, some of them retaining hardly the faintest semblance to Christianity? Can you find the Christianity of the world anywhere except as identified, with that one great world-wide organisation, the centre of which is Rome? Take Rome out of the world, and where is Christendom? Take away the one universal Roman Church, and I ask you, where is Christianity? Then, if the history of Christianity is the history of the Christian Church, what is the history of the Christian Church but the history of the Holy See? Will the history of the Church in England, or the history of the Church in Gaul, or the history of the Church in Spain, suffice to set before us the action of the Church of God in the world, if you blot out the history of the Holy See? In writing the history of the Holy See, the head, the light, the guide, the legislator, the prince of the whole Church, you write the history of all its provinces, as in writing the history of Rome you write the history of the heathen world. And further than this, in writing the history of the Holy See, you write the history of the Pontiffs. It is not the material seat, whether of bronze or of stone, which may crumble into dust, that constitutes the See of Peter. It is the person, it is the man, it is the successor of Peter, it is the Vicar of Jesus Christ, that constitutes the Holy See; and the history of the Holy See is the history of a succession of men, two hundred and fifty and more, who link us now with the day when "the Word was made flesh" and was visible among mankind—

that long line of living witnesses and of Supreme Pontiffs who have ruled the world. The history then of the Holy See is the history of the Church; the history of civilisation is the history of the Pontiffs. Where, I would ask, are there princes, philosophers, statesmen, or conquerors, who have contributed to Christian Europe what St. Leo the Great, St. Gregory the Great, St. Gregory VII., Gregory XI., Innocent III., Alexander III., Sixtus V., and St. Pius V. effected? The worst that can be said is this, that in that line of two hundred and fifty Supreme Pontiffs, there have been a few who have descended to the level of temporal sovereigns. But except those few, they have been the legislators and the rulers, the civilisers and the creators, of the civil order of Europe, under the shelter of which we live. My last remark, then, is this: we live in a day in which a man who stands up to defend the temporal power of the Pope, and the government of the Roman State, is ridiculed and scorned as a lover of despotism, of darkness, of popular ignorance, and of popular oppression. I am not indeed a politician; for when I became a servant of our divine Lord, unworthy as I am to bear the priesthood, I renounced politics; but I have my convictions about civil and political rights, and the man who thinks me a lover of despotism and darkness does not know me. Nevertheless I will dare to say this, that the Roman state is, in its very essence, the freest and most republican and the most popular in Christian Europe. And this paradox I will prove. It is the only elective monarchy under the sun. It is the only elective throne that has ever endured. Poland for two hundred years elected its kings, and perished in confusion. The Roman state for eighteen hundred years has elected its own princes, and it endures. There sits upon the throne of the Roman state a man chosen freely, chosen by election. And further, another principle pervades that government which exists in no other in the world—that the man who sits upon the throne may be any one among the subjects of the state. There is not a man born within the frontier of the Roman state who is not eligible for the office of Supreme Pontiff. There was a time when our forefathers were under the oppression of the Normans. The poor Saxon was then ground down under the heel of the conquering race; when suddenly upon the throne of the Supreme Pontiff there sat one Nicholas Breakspear, a poor Saxon; and the kings and princes of Europe, even the Norman Conqueror, kissed the feet of the poor Saxon, because he reigned as Vicar of Jesus Christ. The whole Saxon population of England was raised when a poor unknown man, a son of a race trodden down under oppression and contempt, was elevated to be, in his Divine Master's name, King of kings and Lord of lords. In the

Roman state, at this moment, there is not a man, though the son of a peasant, who may not be Pope. In the history of the Popes there are many instances of the sons of the poorest in the land who have risen to be Supreme Pontiffs. History tells us of one who, when his mother came to salute him on his elevation, dressed in the attire of a lady, said to her, "Mother, I do not know you; I knew you only in your peasant's garb; go and put on that old dress I love so well: I shall know my mother then." He sent her from his presence; but when she came back in her peasant garb embraced her. The Sovereign Pontiffs are elected from the ecclesiastical order, and the ecclesiastical order is open to every man in the state. There is not a man that may not be a priest; the only conditions are these: he must renounce the world; he must not seek riches; he must not live for himself; he must live years of study, and pass a life of no slight mortification; he shall not seek to lay the foundations of a family; but he shall aim at a higher standard of virtue; and shall try to be, both intellectually and morally, fitted for so great a dignity as to consecrate the Body and Blood of Jesus Christ: and out of men who are thus raised and trained, formed and ripened, to be fitted to consecrate the precious Body and Blood of our Lord upon the altar—out of these the Supreme Pontiff is elected.

But this is the government of priests; which is a

detestable and degrading clog on the progress of civilisation. And yet it was the government of priests that created modern Europe. It is the government of priests that now, for twelve hundred years, has reigned over the fair fabric of Christendom. Compare it with the government of laymen. Never was there a Pontiff who made one offensive war. There is not a square foot of his patrimony which he obtained by bloodshed. Talk of the government of laymen: look at the empires, look at the kingdoms, of modern Europe; look at the condition of the people; read their history; if they are somewhat better now, what were they but a little while ago? What was this country in the last century? The government of priests need fear no comparison with that of laymen. But I have brought the subject as far as I possibly can at this time. There are many other things I would fain say, but I must conclude, and I will conclude simply with these words. You remember when, in the council of Jerusalem, a prudent man stood up and gave this advice to the Sanhedrim: "Refrain from these men, and let them alone: for if this design, or work, be of men, it will fall to nothing."* Now I say to any one who feels a desire to oppose the temporal power of the Pope, Lay no hand on that man; for if this counsel or this work be of man, it will utterly come

* Acts v. 38.

to naught, nay, it will break and be dissipated in the air, in the dust and confusion of all human works. But if it be not of man, if it be of God,—and the world has been waiting for eighteen hundred years for the fall of the spiritual sovereignty, and at least twelve hundred for the fall of the civil sovereignty of Rome, to see if the test of Gamaliel would have effect,—take heed, " lest perhaps you be found even to fight against God." *

* Acts v. 39.

LECTURE III.

If what I have already said be true, what I have to say in the present Lecture may perhaps seem almost unnecessary. If it be true that the temporal power of the Popes has been a providential instrument, whereby God has created Christian Europe, then certainly the destruction of that providential instrument must bring with it the dissolution of the work, which has not only been created, but supported and sustained by it to this day. I might, therefore, be content to rest upon the proofs already adduced; for if they be good, the converse hardly need be proved; if they be not good, that which I have now to say would be irrelevant. But it is for those who object, to show cause why they should not be admitted. In truth I do not know how anybody, without denying the Divine origin and mission of Christianity itself, can deny these principles, for they are simple, broad, and self-evident, partly by revelation, and partly by history. As I have said, all that I assume is, belief in the Incarnation and in a visible Church.

The subject upon which I have now to speak,

namely, the dissolution of the temporal power of the Popes, raises in my mind a previous question, whether indeed this temporal power, until the second coming of our Lord Jesus Christ, shall ever be dissolved? I do not say it ever will; for when I look at history, I find that the same events which are under our eyes at this moment have been enacted and re-enacted, produced and reproduced, over and over again, with the change only in the names of those who have invaded the patrimony of St. Peter, and of the Sovereign Pontiffs who have resisted the invasion. The whole history of Christian Europe presents a succession of attacks and usurpations upon the patrimony of the Church, followed again by the recognition and the restoration of the same temporal sovereignty. Therefore I do not mean to say that the day will ever come when the menaces and the intrigues of those in power shall succeed in displacing this providential fact of God. Yet the event may come to pass, that as our divine Lord, after His three years of public ministry were ended, delivered Himself of His own free will into the hands of men, and thereby permitted them to do that which before was impossible, so, in His inscrutable wisdom, He may deliver over His Vicar upon earth, as He delivered Himself, and that the providential support of the temporal power of the Holy See may be withdrawn when its work is done. What that work is, we know from Holy Scripture;

it is the support and maintenance of the present Christian order of the world, during such time as the grace of God is gathering out His people, until the whole number of those whom He hath chosen to eternal life be filled up. It may be that, when that is done, and that when the times of Antichrist are come, He will give over His Vicar upon earth, and His mystical body at large, for three years and a half to the powers of this world. Now it is not needful to determine or to raise this question; it is enough for me to show that the acts which tend to the dissolution of the temporal power of the Popes likewise tend to the dissolution of Christian Europe; and that they who do such acts with this intention resist the ordinance of God, and purchase judgment for themselves.

I. First of all, therefore, I have to show that the dissolution of this temporal power of the Pope would lead to the dissolution of Christendom, that is, of Christian Europe. Suppose the Vicar of Jesus Christ on earth were to-morrow despoiled of his temporal sovereignty and made subject to some temporal prince; he would, as I have said, so far lose the providential character, by virtue of which he is fulfilling the civil mission of the Church in the world. He would cease to act upon kingdoms, upon monarchies, upon nations, upon people, upon legislatures, upon congresses, and upon conventions. He would cease to act upon the springs of national life, and upon the sources of imperial power. He would cease wholly to deal with the nations, and with the organised life of the world. He and the whole Church would thenceforth, as in the beginning, in the first three hundred years, be concerned solely with individuals. Here and there the grace of God would move them, and the Church would, as in the first ages, be again made up of members voluntarily uniting themselves together throughout the whole world, having indeed a legal recognition here and there, but isolated among the nations, without any contact with the kingdoms of the world as such. The state of the world before Constantine would be reproduced; the Church would descend again, if I may so say, into the Catacombs, and would be hidden from society; it would cease to take its place with the powers of the world, having an existence beside and above them. It would cease to be seen in the councils of princes, in legislatures and parliaments, to have a status in the world; it would have no place in diplomacy as a contracting power, or in the public legislature except to be prohibited. Now it must be evident at once that this deposition of the Vicar of Jesus Christ and of the Church from their relation to the civil powers of the world, would entirely dissolve the bonds and the order of Christian Europe. So clearly is this seen at this moment, that there comes a voice even from schismatical Russia, which has no part in the unity of the Catholic Church, and from the statesmen of schismatical England, who are always in hostility to the Holy See, declaring that such an event would destroy the constituted basis of the civilised order of the Christian world.

II. A further effect would be, to put the civil and spiritual powers in conflict throughout the whole world. The moment the head and centre of Christendom shall have lost his sovereignty, from that moment the Church throughout its whole extension will virtually lose its independence. The moment the Bishop of Rome is reduced to the condition of the Archbishop of Paris or the Archbishop of Vienna, the civil supremacy which presses upon them would be redoubled in its weight. They would have no support upon which they could fall back. They would be treated as the Archbishop of Canterbury or the Patriarchs of Moscow; the latter indeed having now no person to represent the office, which is vested by commission in what is called the œcumenical synod, chiefly composed of the imperial family of Russia. The moment the civil supremacy of the Church is overturned, then the Church in all the kingdoms of the earth, instead of standing as it does now in the relation of independence to the civil powers of Europe, would immediately be regarded as subject.

The effect of this would be, first of all, an uneasy relation of jealousy, undefined limits of jurisdiction, claims and counter claims, interference and clashing of tribunals and judgments—between the spiritual and civil powers: a condition of things which existed for centuries before the Reformation in England, and which has continued in certain parts of the Continent; as, for instance, in France, during the contests of the Gallican liberties, as they are called, or Gallican servitudes, as they might be more rightly named; in Portugal in the last century; in Austria under Joseph the Second, when the two powers were in continual variance, always jealous, and always in conflict. Then comes a crisis. What, in fact, was the Reformation in England under Henry VIII. but simply a crisis in this conflict? And after the crisis, there would in the end come a system of penal laws, more unrelenting, more sanguinary, more merciless, more refined than the world has ever seen; for modern legislatures have acquired a subtilty, a keenness of instinct, and a power of accomplishing what that keen instinct dictates, which was unknown in the ruder times of persecution. Witness the penal laws of England, and still more the penal laws of Ireland, for there is not in all the legislation of the world anything more terrible than the Irish penal laws. I will not now stay to narrate what they were; any one who desires to know them may read them in a very common book—Brennan's *History of the Church in Ireland*. Anything more hateful, or more godless, than some of those penal statutes, the history of the world cannot show. This, however, is the legitimate result of a conflict between the spiritual and temporal powers : it begins with an uneasy jealousy—it may be a conflict in Vienna or in Paris, as in the last century, which, carried to its legitimate consequence, ends in a system of penal laws, by which the spiritual power is again reduced to a state of bondage; or in a persecution of 1793.

III. The third effect of the dissolution of the temporal sovereignty of the Popes is one to which I think the politicians of this world and the people who love liberty will do well to look. The moment the spiritual power is subjected to the temporal, comes that worst form of human government, an unlimited despotism. The only limitation and check upon the abuse of temporal power is the independence of the spiritual; the spiritual power, being independent of the civil, stands by the throne of princes, to restrain them from excesses of their authority. If you wish to find despotism, look at Sweden, Denmark, and England during the high times of Protestant ascendency. If you wish for an authority for this, read one least liable to suspicion. Laing, in his *Notes on Europe* and *on Sweden*, which are two distinct books, gives facts which satisfactorily prove that it is in Protestant countries especially that monarchies have become despotic ; and that wheresoever in Catholic countries the old traditionary limitations of the civil power, by their relations to the spiritual, have been preserved, there monarchy has always been mitigated. It is a significant fact, that the power which at the present moment is in open conflict with the sovereignty of the Holy See is, at this very time, exercising a repression on all popular movements, all intellect, all will, all thought, all speech in its legislative assemblies, in the freedom of its press, in the action of private persons, in the expression of their opinions, such as I know not to exist in any other country in Europe. I believe that it is a certain fact in history, that in proportion as the spiritual power in any country is depressed, the despotism of the temporal power rises; and in proportion as the sovereignty of the spiritual power is elevated, the despotism of the temporal power is held in check.

IV. The fourth effect would be to let loose an irresistible spirit of revolution; for violent repressions of the popular will are surely followed by equally strong reactions and counteractions. From the despotism of the old French monarchy, the first French Revolution was the natural, inevitable recoil. And we may regard it as certain, that the history of Europe will hereafter have to record that which it has recorded before in a similar instance. Of this point, however, I say no more.

Now it may be asked, is, then, all revolution unlawful? To which I answer by asking, is all homicide unlawful? No man will say that homicide is always lawful, and no man will say that homicide is never lawful; no man will ever say that warfare is always lawful, and no man will say that warfare is never lawful. It is certain that if a man seeks my life, I may take his in self-defence. It is certain that if a kingdom makes war upon another, the latter may take up arms in self-defence. And such a homicide and such a warfare would not only be lawful, but would be just. There are cases, therefore, in which homicide may be lawful, and in which war may be lawful: but war and homicide are only lawful exceptionally, and unless justified by their occasion are absolutely unlawful. Now what is this exception? It is lawful to use self-defence to protect life; nature has implanted it in man, nature has bestowed it on society. What is warfare but the privilege and principle of self-defence, used against an external enemy? For which reason, all defensive wars are lawful, but no offensive war is lawful. No war of mere aggression, of mere conquest, can be lawful; but a war of self-defence is always lawful. A war of self-defence may be of two kinds; it may be either the repulse of an attack, or it may be the anticipation of hostilities. If a man approaches me armed with a deadly weapon, and I know with moral certainty that one moment will forfeit my life, I am justified in taking his, that is in anticipating the act of aggression. So, if one kingdom or people knew that another was hovering upon its frontier with an armed force, which would certainly descend upon it like an inundation, that people would be justified in arming its legions and going out to war. War, therefore, which is against a foreign enemy may be lawful. What, then, is the rule with regard to internal war? Suppose a prince were to become the enemy of his people, and were to levy war upon them; if he were to take their lives, and the lives of their children; such a people would be justified in protecting themselves by the primary law of nature. There is no doubt that if a prince were to put himself out of the pale of civil and political life, by threatening his people in such a way that they knew it to be a mere question of time when he should commence a sanguinary and fatal attack upon them, they would be justified in preventing it. The Church has again and again recognised the lawfulness and justice of such a proceeding: for the judgment of a whole people, the common sense of a Christian nation, is an instinct so high, that in the ordinary course of history we hardly ever find it wrong; and those princes who have been hurled from their thrones by the judgments of the Supreme Pontiffs, such as Philip I. of France, Henry IV. of Germany, Frederick II. of

Germany, were tyrants already denounced by the mass of their people, on account of the wrongs they had committed. I do not say, therefore, that there never can come to pass a case in which a people in self-defence may be justified in protecting themselves from acts on the part of their rulers, of so grave and injurious a nature as to involve in fact the life and the moral and social well-being of the people; but this I say, that unless a revolution can be justified by causes as grave as those which I have defined, whereby it puts off the character of a revolution, and puts on the character of a judicial process and of a solemn and public legislative act, by the will of the people at large, I know of no plea that can clear a revolution of guilt in the sight of God. I believe that every revolution which is made for a light cause, and every revolution which is made for a superficial cause, comes under the sentence of the Holy Ghost, in the words of the Apostle with which I began, that "He that resisteth the power resisteth the ordinance of God, and shall have purchased judgment for himself."

Now let me apply this to the subject which is before us. We are told, that a large part of the dominions of the Holy Father is in revolution: I ask, then, is this a revolution which is justifiable? or is this a rebellion? Let us inquire into the causes.

But before I speak of these in detail, I cannot

refrain from saying one word upon the state of public credulity in England. England, a most cultivated and enlightened nation, a nation so literary that it is every day deluged with newspapers, which it reads as it would read a shower of gospels, is of all the nations of Europe the most credulous. I hardly know one that is so readily and so easily deceived as England. And what makes it the more wonderful is this, that other nations, which have not the same profuse freedom of communication, are deceived with their eyes either shut or but half-open; while England is deceived with its eyes open, with the whole flood of the light of the newspaper press upon it; and it is deceived into believing things so profoundly absurd, so far from fact or truth, that nothing but a disposition of the will to believe that which it reads can account for it. It reminds me of a picture which I saw publicly exhibited last year. It made a great impression upon me. It was a beautiful painting, representing two boys, one with his hands clenched, with contracted features, and with a storm of passion lowering on his brow. Though he was represented as being but twelve or thirteen years of age, or even less, he appeared to have all the intensity, all the earnestness of Italy, in her present depressed state, working in his intellect and in his heart. He was a picture of misery, of bitterness, of animosity, and of resentment. By his side stood a fair boy, with all the ease and flexibility of youth, broad and vigorously built, with an open countenance, exhibiting the aspect of an English boy, full of freedom, full of sunshine, full of joy. This was the contrast of Italy and England; no doubt those that saw it believed that they had here an exact picture of the peasantry in the Roman States—poor, miserable, degraded, tortured, embittered. I would that I could bring before those that look upon such a picture what I have myself continually seen; a little Roman peasant boy, perhaps twelve years old, with the quiet self-possession, with the courage and fearlessness of a man, with a long ox-goad driving a bullock or buffalo along the road, exhibiting the vigour, I may say, of manhood—a traditional type of the race whose name he bears. Or see these same children on the side of some gentle knoll in the Campagna, playing together with a spirit of joy such as is seldom found in poor English village children; or watch them, it may be, kneeling by the way-side with head uncovered, saying their rosary or their prayers before some shrine of devotion; and then compare them with the poor, sallow, shrunken boys whom we see day by day in the streets of London, in the hands of the police, going first to the prison and then to the reformatory, for stealing, it may be, a broken bottle or a crust of bread. Now I say that my picture is equally truthful; and if I were to paint this and have it exhibited, all the English world would rise up in a flame of indignation, and would denounce me as false. I say, in like manner, the other picture was a falsehood. Nevertheless, it is an exact illustration of the perpetual caricatures made of the Roman states in the public newspapers of England. I can compare such accounts to nothing but to a history published in Constantinople in the time of Belisarius. In the midst of the high refinement and education of the Byzantine court, there was an historian who said that in Britain (it was our turn then) there was a province within which the land was uninhabitable, because covered with serpents, and the atmosphere so poisonous that no man could breathe it and live; and that night by night to this province of Britain the dead from the continent of Europe were conveyed by a race of seamen who were fishermen, and that the seamen felt their boats depressed in the water by the weight of the souls they carried. They heard the dead men speak, but never saw their forms.* This was believed at that day in Constantinople, as these representations of the Roman states are believed now in England. I will venture to say there is not a subject upon which the English people are more profoundly misinformed than the actual internal condition of the Roman states. If a revolutionist writes a book, as a certain Farini did, one of our statesmen can be found to translate it into

Macaulay's History of England, vol. i. p. 5.

English. In that book will be found a wholly one-sided report of all which can be said against Rome in regard to taxes, duties on salt, detention of prisoners, and the like; and then the English people, who are immersed in details of this sort, imagine that this constitutes a condition of misgovernment intolerable to a Christian people.

Now I shall not be too bold if I say that the causes of the present revolution in the States of the Church are to be found not from within, but from without. They do not arise from any springs of bitterness which are native to the soil. The cause of the present state of that country I believe to be this. First of all, by long tradition, an animosity and a hostility has been cherished in, and by means of, the secret societies which date from the Middle Ages. We in England, in our insular unconsciousness of the state of foreign countries, read of these secret societies as a thing of the past. There they live, they are in full activity, in full intelligence, in full communication at this moment, as they were in ages past. Next, the theory of political society, which is the consequence of the Protestant Reformation, and in particular the right of popular insurrection, and the rejection of any external arbitration or judgment between peoples and their princes, has already affected the whole political state of Europe. It has passed over Germany, over France, over England, and over Spain, and has now descended into Italy. Thirdly, the infidelity of Voltaire, and of the great French school founded by him and his companions, penetrated largely into Italy in the last century. Then the revolution of 1793 in France set the revolutionary principle in motion, which penetrated the whole length of the Italian peninsula. Again, the invasion by the French under the first Napoleon deluged Italy anew with the French revolutionary spirit. All the municipal institutions of the traditional Roman government, all that which had constituted the free government of the Roman states from the Middle Ages downwards, were suddenly abolished, and the Code Napoléon imposed instead. Again, there has been an active co-operation from the beginning of the present century of the modern revolutionary societies, and they have made the Roman states the focus of their conspiracies. Once more, the disaffected from every part, not of Italy alone, but of France and Germany, and of England to her shame, have congregated in Rome and in the Roman states. Further, the war in the beginning of the last year has had its effects. We, in our simplicity, imagine that Italy was as calm and tranquil when the whole of its North was shaken by the concussion of a mighty conflict as Yorkshire or as Scotland We are so utterly unused to the effects of continental movements, and so little understand how one continental nation is affected by another,—for our four seas so gird us round,—that we cannot conceive how the influence of the war in Lombardy should have penetrated everywhere in the Roman state. Then there were armies hovering on its frontiers; there were distributions of arms among its people; there were inflammatory proclamations and incitements of every kind scattered broadcast among its population; there were emissaries of foreign countries, intrigues the most unscrupulous. Portions of the Roman population were organised, trained, and disciplined to arms by officers of the kingdom of Sardinia. I ask, do you require further reasons why a portion of the Holy Father's states are in opposition to him? It is because the whole flood of external revolution has found its home there, and because of the flagrant ambition of neighbouring states.

Now I ask you, is this a condition in which revolution is justified by the principles I have laid down in the beginning? Has the Sovereign Pontiff levied war upon his subjects? Has he threatened the life of any man? Whose shoe-latchet, whose ox, or whose ass, has he taken? Can he not, in the words of the man of God, the man Moses, the meekest of men upon earth, put his people to the test, and ask whom he has wronged? Where, then, is the justification for a movement such as this? I ask further, if this stimulus to revolution had been applied to Canada,—if those who hovered about its frontiers some years ago had been aided by all these causes of revolution, —would Canada be British now? If the same had been tried in 1798, or in 1848, upon a country nearer to the shores of England, nay, I say upon an English county, though it were the royal county of Cornwall, they would not have resisted causes of rebellion like these, nor would they have retained their loyalty and allegiance to the crown of England. I say, then, it is hypocrisy, when the public events of the world and the public history of Europe give the reasons of this rebellion, to cast the blame of it upon him who is blameless. Any man who knows the character of Pius IX., any man who has read his history, has watched his acts, knows that since his pontificate not one man has died for political offences; while the lives even of many who have been taken in homicide have been spared by him, and their punishments commuted to imprisonment. If the prisons are full, it is because offences which in England are avenged with capital punishment are there treated in a milder way. The very mildness of the Roman law multiplies its prisoners, and then Europe rises up and cries out on the state of the Roman prisons. I might go on; I might add many instances. But it is enough for me to say that I challenge any man to show a cause to justify the rebellion of any portion of the Roman state, which would not, at the same time, not only justify the United States in the War of Independence—which British statesmen then so loudly and eloquently denounced—but would justify every English colony in resisting the legislature of the mother country. I would ask any man to show any cause to justify the rising of any portion of the Pope's dominions, which would not at the same time set in motion the unlimited principle of revolution in all nations.

V. The last point upon which I would speak is this, the end of this conflict with the Catholic Church will be to desecrate the civil powers of the world. So long as they continue in a relation of amity with the Christian Church by which they were created, they themselves continue Christian and are consecrated; the moment they revolt from it they desecrate themselves. By a desecrated power I mean a power which does not acknowledge any form of faith as an obligation upon its conscience. Now look at Protestant countries; look, for instance, at our own. What is the form of faith which is held in England to be binding upon the conscience of the English people? Not the Established Church; for that is not infallible. At the Reformation it was declared that the Church of England might err; and therefore its religion cannot be binding upon the conscience. It may be binding by law, and most sanguinary laws were made to bind it upon the consciences of Englishmen; and what has been their effect? More than one half of the whole

English population is in dissent, following every form of contradictory Christianity. And of the Established Church itself, which of its many forms of Christian opinion does the law of the land make obligatory on its ministers or its people? We see at this moment that every form of contradiction prevails in it; a state of things producing doubt, scepticism, infidelity, hatred of Christianity. There I see a civil power desecrated. Now I will not dwell on other examples. France, after the Revolution of 1830, declared by its first organic articles that there was no state religion; France, therefore, has desecrated itself. The mass of the French people, being Catholic, remain in union with the Holy See, and are still upholders of Christian order. But the civil power of France is desecrated. Next, in regard to morals. In the year 1793 the old Christian and Catholic law of marriage was abolished in France, and the law of divorce was admitted. Within three months of that one year, the divorces were 570, and the whole number of marriages in Paris during the whole twelve months of that year was 1700. That is, the divorces were more than one-third compared with the marriages. What has been the moral condition of that people, I leave history to say. I should not quote this, if it were not to drive home a fact which the last two years have recorded in the statutes of England. Marriage up to that year was indissoluble in England. Marriage in England is indissoluble no longer, except for those who are in union with the Holy See. The only witness for the indissolubleness of marriage, which is the root of civil society, the foundation of domestic life, the fountain and source of all the sanctities and purities of the world,—that which, I will say, next after the institution of the Church itself, is the cause and principle of all that is holy upon earth, the sole and only witness in the world that testifies to it, is the Church of Rome. The schismatical Greek has given it up; the schismatical Protestant has given it up. It is a step towards the license of that greater apostasy, the apostasy of Mahomet. The sole and only guardian of morals in the world is the one, holy, Catholic, and Roman Church, represented and impersonated in the Supreme Pontiff.

When the civil powers of the world shall desecrate themselves and lose their relation to Christianity, they will inaugurate the beginning of the last times, when Antichrist shall come. It was foretold by a holy father, St. Hippolytus, that before the end of the world, the Roman empire would be broken up into ten democracies, and that paganism would be restored. How shall we interpret this strange prophecy? The facts of the modern world give us the interpretation. Natural society, which when once subjugated by the providence of God became Christian Europe, will again break forth. It will resume its powers of unregenerated and unchastened will and passion, and men will constitute a society which is not of God. Christian Europe is God's society; but society without faith is the society of man, the antagonist of God. "That which is born of the flesh, is flesh; that which is born of the Spirit, is spirit." * There is an irreconcilable conflict between these two principles. Do not you think that I am extravagant, and going out of all bounds and measure in what I say. What, I ask you, was the first French Revolution but paganism revived? What was the Garibaldian rising in 1848 but old heathenism, which had been subdued in Italy and Rome, and held under by the Christian order of Europe, striving once more for the ascendency, with its impiety, its infidelity, its blasphemy against God?

This is the end to which the fair structure of Christian Europe seems tending. I do not say it will ever arrive at this end, for the providence of God may indeed check its course. Of this I know nothing. But of this I am sure, if I see two lines drawn apparently parallel, and yet converging by no more than a hair's-breadth, though they should reach to a distance far beyond the horizon, I could predict with the certainty of an inspired man that those converging lines must meet. If I see certain great antichristian principles in motion throughout Europe, I

* St. John iii. 6.

need no inspiration, no gift of prophecy, to say that, give those principles and movements time to work out their result, that result must be the destruction of the Christian society of Europe, and the restoration of the natural society of man without God in the world.

Now I have said all that I can at this time; and with one word I will conclude. They who lend a hand to this work of destruction, they who speak a word for it, they who sympathise with it, are all against God, and will purchase to themselves judgment according to their proportion. What their proportion may be, I know not.

That judgment will be in this world and in the next. Read the history of Christian Europe, and look along the line of its monarchs who have contended with the Vicar of Christ, and find me one who has ever contended against the temporal sovereignty of the Vicar of our divine Lord, and has not been chastised. Find me one who has ever dared to resist the divine ordinance of God, in whose history there is not written—nay scored, in characters so deep that the lapse of ages cannot efface them—the judgment of God upon that rebellious head. I will not go to old examples; I will take only one fresh in these days. There was one who rose to a zenith of power in Europe which has never been surpassed. The whole of France was under his feet; his arms had won the dominion of Spain; Germany had been beaten down again and again in a succession of battles. He had been crowned King of Italy. There was a king of Rome of his own making; Belgium was his; Sweden was reigned over by his creature; England alone remained, as it were, floating on the waves, and was one last home of freedom defended by its own waters. These were the only barriers to his universal rule. But in the zenith of his power he saw an old defenceless man in the Vatican, whom, most unchivalrously, his armed men hurried away in the dead of the night. Weak and sick as he was, they hurried him along, with the blinds of his carriage down, lest whosoever should see him should recognise him to be the Vicar of Christ. That poor feeble prey was in the grasp of the eagle; he was imprisoned at Savona and at Fontainebleau. This great Emperor was king of the world; and when this lonely feeble man affixed to the doors of his church the sentence of excommunication, the Emperor said, "Does he think this will make the muskets fall from the hands of my soldiers?"—"Within three short years," as an historian, and himself a soldier in that great and terrible expedition, writes, "our men could not hold their muskets." You know the history; that which has been shall be.

I urge you, therefore, think with the Church; live with the Church; let your whole heart and soul, every thought of your intellect, every affection of your heart, every emotion of your will, be with the Church of God. The Church of God is the presence of God, and the mind of the Church is the mind of God, and the voice of the Church is the voice of God. Next, love the person of the Vicar of Christ—not as an abstract principle, not the Holy See, not an institution, but the living breathing man, who has upon him the dignity and the unction of the Great High Priest. Be filially devoted to him; for the time is come when, according to the prophecy, he is the sign which shall be spoken against; he is set for the fall and for the rising again of nations. He is the test of the world; Pius IX., that despised name to those who are not of his family, is sifting the nations. And there are voices coming up now as of old, "Hail, King of the Jews!" and they would fain blindfold him, and buffet him, and spit upon his face. They mock him as a false king with a feeble reed, as an impotent king with a crown of thorns. They offer the mock loyalty of a revolting people, and they say, "Away with him! we will not have this man to reign over us; we have no king but Cæsar." But he is Vicar of Him who will judge the world.

PART SECOND.

The Perpetual Conflict of the Vicar of Jesus Christ.

LECTURE I.

I AM well aware that the truths and principles of Revelation have been, by the common consent of public men, formally excluded from the sphere of politics, and that to apply them as tests to the events of the world is regarded, in these days, as a weakness of mind. They who reject Revelation altogether are consistent in such a judgment; but with what consistency they who profess to believe in a revelation of the Divine government of the world, nevertheless consent to exclude it from the field of contemporaneous history, I cannot tell. I am therefore going, *prudens et videns,* to run counter to the popular spirit of these times, and it may be to expose myself to the contempt or compassion of those who believe the world to be governed by the action of the human will alone. To this I resign myself very willingly, and with no perturbation. My intention is, to examine the present relation of the Church to the civil powers of the world, by the light of a prophecy recorded by St. Paul, and to draw out certain principles of a practical kind for the direction of those who believe that the Divine will is also present in the events now taking place before our eyes.

I am not about to enter upon expositions of the Apocalypse, or to calculate the year of the end of the world. This I leave to those who may be called to it. The points I propose to take are few and practical; and the result I desire to attain is a clearer discernment of what principles are Christian, and what are Antichristian, and a surer appreciation of the character of the events by which the Church and the Holy See are at present tried.

St. Paul, writing to the Thessalonians, says: " Let no man deceive you by any means: for unless there come a revolt first, and the man of sin be revealed, the son of perdition, who opposeth, and is lifted up above all that is called God, or that is worshipped, so that he sitteth in the temple of God, showing himself as if he were God. Remember you not, that when I was yet with you, I told you these things ? And now you know what withholdeth, that he may be revealed in his time. For the mystery of iniquity already worketh: only that he who now holdeth, do hold, until he be taken out of the way, and then that wicked one shall be revealed, whom the Lord Jesus shall kill with the spirit of his mouth, and shall destroy with the brightness of his coming: him, whose coming is according to the working of Satan, in all power, and signs, and lying wonders, and in all seduction of iniquity to them that perish: because they received not the love of the truth, that they might be saved. Therefore God shall send them the operation of error, to believe lying: that all may be judged who have not believed the truth, but have consented to iniquity."*

We have here a prophecy of four great facts: first, of a *revolt*, which shall precede the second coming of our Lord; secondly, of the *manifestation* of one who is called "the wicked one;" thirdly, of a *hindrance*, which restrains his manifestation; and lastly, of the *period of power and persecution*, of which he will be the author.

In treating of this subject, I shall not venture upon any conjectures of my own, but shall deliver simply what I find either in the Fathers of the Church, or in such theologians as the Church has recognised, namely, Bellarmine, Lessius, Malvenda, Viegas, Suarez, Ribera, and others.

First, then, what is the revolt? In the original it is called ἀποστασία, "an apostasy;" and in the Vulgate, *discessio*, or "a departure." Now a revolt implies a seditious separation from some authority, and a consequent opposition to it.

If we can find the authority, we shall find perhaps also the revolt.

* 2 Thess. ii. 3-11.

Now there are in the world but two ultimate authorities, the civil and the spiritual, and this revolt must be either a sedition or a schism. Moreover, it must be something upon a wide field, and in proportion to the terms and events of the prediction.

St. Jerome, with some others, interprets this revolt to be the rebellion of the nations or provinces against the Roman Empire. He says, "Nisi venerit discessio . . . ut omnes gentes, quæ Romano Imperio subjacent, recedant ab eo;"[*] an interpretation we need not examine, forasmuch as the events of Christian history refute it. They have revolted, and no manifestation has appeared. It seems to need little proof that this revolt or apostasy is a separation, not from the civil, but from the spiritual order and authority; for the sacred writers, again and again, speak of such a spiritual separation; and in one place St. Paul seems expressly to declare the meaning of this word. He forewarns St. Timothy that in the later days, τινὲς ἀποστήσονται ἀπὸ τῆς πίστεως, "some shall depart or apostatise from the faith;" and it seems evident that the same spiritual falling away is intended by the apostasy in this place.

The authority, then, from which the revolt is to take place is that of the kingdom of God on earth, prophesied by Daniel as the kingdom which the God of heaven should set up, after the four kingdoms

[*] S. Hier. Ep. ad Algasiam.

should be destroyed by the stone cut out without hands, which became a great mountain and filled the whole earth; or, in other words, the one and universal Church, founded by our Divine Lord, and spread by His Apostles throughout the world. In this one only supernatural kingdom was deposited the true and pure theism, or knowledge of God, and the true and only faith of God incarnate, with the doctrines and laws of grace. This, then, is the authority from which the revolt is to be made, be that revolt what it may.

Such being the authority against which the revolt is made, it cannot be difficult to ascertain its character. The inspired writers expressly describe its notes.

The first is, schism, as given by St. John: "It is the last hour: and as you have heard that Antichrist cometh: even now there are become many Antichrists: whereby we know that it is the last hour. They went out from us; but they were not of us. For if they had been of us, they would no doubt have remained with us."*

The second note is, the rejection of the office and presence of the Holy Ghost. St. Jude says, "These are they, who separate themselves, sensual men" (*i.e.* ψυχικοί, animal or merely rational and natural men), "having not the spirit."† This necessarily involves

* 1 St. John ii. 18, 19.   † St. Jude 19.

the heretical principle of human opinion as opposed to Divine faith; of the private spirit as opposed to the infallible voice of the Holy Spirit, speaking through the Church of God.

The third note is, the denial of the Incarnation. St. John writes, " Every spirit which confesseth that Jesus Christ is come in the flesh is of God: and every spirit that dissolveth Jesus " (that is, by denying the mystery of the Incarnation, either the true Godhead, or the true manhood, or the unity or divinity of the person of the Incarnate Son) " is not of God, and this is Antichrist, of whom you have heard that he cometh, and he is now already in the world."*—Again he says, " Many seducers are gone out into the world, who confess not that Jesus Christ is come in the flesh : this is a seducer and an Antichrist." †

These, then, are the marks by which, as the Church is to be known by her notes, the antichristian revolt, or apostasy, may be distinguished. We will now see whether they can be verified in the history of Christianity, or in the present position of the Church in the world.

The first point to notice is, that both St. Paul and St. Peter speak of this antichristian revolt as already begun in their own day.

St. Paul says, " The mystery of iniquity already

* St. John iv. 2, 3. † 2 Epis. 7.

worketh: only that he who now holdeth do hold, until he be taken out of the way."* And St. John expressly, in the above-quoted places: "It is the last hour: and as you have heard that Antichrist cometh, even now there are become many Antichrists: whereby we know that it is the last hour."† Again, "This is Antichrist, of whom you have heard that he cometh, and he is now already in the world."‡

We must look, then, for the beginnings of this revolt in the times of the Apostles. The spirit of Antichrist was at work as soon as Christ was manifested to the world. In one word, therefore, it describes the continuous working of the spirit of heresy, which from the beginning has run parallel to the faith.

It is evident that St. Paul and St. John applied these terms to the Nicolaitans, the Gnostics, and the like. The three notes of Antichrist, schism, heresy, and the denial of the Incarnation, were manifest in them. It is also applicable to the Sabellian, Arian, Semiarian, Monophysite, Monothelite, Eutychian, and Macedonian heresies. The principles are identical; the development various, but only accidental. And so, throughout these eighteen hundred years, every successive heresy has generated schism, and every schism has generated heresy; and all alike deny the

---

* 2 Thess. ii. 7. † 1 St. John ii. 18.
‡ 1 St. John v. 3.

Divine Voice of the Holy Ghost speaking continuously through the Church; and all alike substitute human opinion for Divine faith; and all alike work out, by a sure process, some more rapidly, and some more slowly, a denial of the Incarnation of the Eternal Son. Some may start with it in the outset, others resolve themselves into it by a long and unforeseen transmutation, as that of Protestantism into Rationalism; but all being identical in principle, are identical also in their consequences. Every age has its heresy, as every article of faith by denial receives its definition; and the course of heresy is measured and periodical; various materially, but formally one, both in principle and in action; so that all the heresies from the beginning are no more than the continuous development and expansion of "the mystery of iniquity," which was already at work.

Another phenomenon in the history of heresy is its power of organising and perpetuating itself, at least until it resolves itself into some more subtil and aggressive form: for instance, Arianism, which rivalled the Catholic Church in Constantinople, Lombardy, and Spain; Donatism, which equalled the Church in Africa; Nestorianism, which outnumbered the Church in Asia; Mahometanism, which punished and absorbed most of its forerunners, and established, in the East and South, the most terrible antichristian military power the world has ever seen; and

Protestantism, which has organised itself into a vast political antagonist to the Holy See, not only in the North, but, by its policy and diplomacy, even in Catholic countries.

To this power of expansion must be added a certain morbid and noxious reproduction. Physiologists tell us that there is a perfect ultimate unity even in the countless diseases which devour the body; nevertheless, each disease seems to throw out its progeny by a corruption and reproduction. So in the history and development of heresy. To name no more than these,—Gnosticism, Arianism, and, above all Protestantism, have generated each a multitude of subordinate and affiliated heresies. But it is Protestantism which, above all others, bears the three notes of the inspired writers in the greatest breadth and evidence. Other heresies have opposed parts and details of the Christian faith and Church; but Protestantism, taken in its historical complex, as we now are able, with the retrospect of three hundred years, to measure it, reaching from the religion of Luther, Calvin, and Cranmer at the one end, to the Rationalism and Pantheism of England and Germany at the other, is of all the most formal, detailed, and commensurate antagonist of Christianity. I do not mean that it has as yet attained its full development, for we shall see reasons to believe that it is still pregnant with a darker future; but even as "the mystery of iniquity has already worked," no other antagonist has as yet gone so deep in undermining the faith of the Christian world.

I am not now pretending to write a treatise on the reproductiveness of Protestantism. It is enough to set down certain facts self-evident in the intellectual history of the last three hundred years, namely, that Socinianism, Rationalism, and Pantheism are the legitimate offspring of the Lutheran and Calvinistic heresies; and that Protestant England, the least consecutive and consistent of Protestant countries, affords at this moment a ready pabulum for the reception and reproduction of these spirits of error.

All that I wish to point out is, to use a modern phrase, that the movement of heresy is one and the same from the beginning; that the Gnostics were the Protestants of their day, and the Protestants the Gnostics of ours; that the principle is identical, and the bulk of the movement unfolded to greater proportions; and its successes accumulated, and its antagonism to the Catholic Church changeless and essential. There are two consequences or operations of this movement so strange and so full of importance, as bearing upon its relation to the Church, that I cannot pass them by.

The first is, the development and worship of the principle of nationality, which has always been found in combination with heresy.

Now, the Incarnation abolished all national distinctions within the sphere of grace, and the Church absorbed all nations into its supernatural unity. One Fountain of spiritual jurisdiction, and one Divine Voice, held together the wills and actions of a family of nations. Sooner or later, every heresy has identified itself with the nation in which it arose. It has lived by the support of civil powers, and they have embodied the claim of national independence.

This movement, which is the key of the so-called great Western schism, is the *rationale* also of the Reformation; and the last three hundred years have given a development and intensity to the spirit of separate nationalism, of which we as yet see no more than the preludes. I need not point out how this nationalism is essentially schismatical. This is to be seen not only in the Anglican Reformation, but in the Gallican liberties, and the contentions of Portugal in Europe and in India, to name no more.

Now I have pointed out this result of heresy because it verifies one of the three marks above-mentioned. If heresy in the individual dissolves the unity of the Incarnation, heresy in a nation dissolves the unity of the Church, which is built upon the Incarnation. And in this we see a truer and deeper meaning of the words of St. Jerome than he foresaw himself. It is not the revolt of nations from the Roman Empire, but the apostasy of nations from

the kingdom of God, which was set up on its ruins. And this process of national defection, which began openly with the Protestant Reformation, is running its course, as we shall see hereafter, even in nations still nominally Catholic; and the Church is putting off its mediæval character as the mother of nations, returning again into its primitive condition as a society of members scattered among the peoples and cities of the world.

The other result I spoke of as the consequence of the later workings of the heretical spirit is the deification of humanity. This we have before us in two distinct forms, namely, in the Pantheistic and in the Positive philosophies; or rather in the religion of Positivism, the last aberration of Comte.

It would be impossible in this place to give an adequate account of these two final developments of unbelief; to do so would need a treatise. It will be enough to express, in a popular way, the outline of these two forms of antichristian impiety.

I take the expression of the Pantheism of Germany from two of its modern expositors, in whom it may be said to culminate. We are told that, "Before the time when creation began, we may imagine that an infinite mind, an infinite essence, or an infinite thought (for here all these are one), filled the universe of space. This, then, as the self-existent One, must be the only absolute reality; all else can be but a developing of the one original and eternal being. . . . This primary essence is not . . . an infinite substance, having the two properties of extension and thought, but an infinite, acting, producing, self-unfolding mind—the living soul of the world." "If we can view all things as the development of the original and absolute principle of life, reason, or being, then it is evident conversely that we may trace the marks of the absolute in everything that exists, and consequently may scan them in the operation of our own minds, as one particular phase of its manifestation."

"In practical philosophy we have three movements: the first is, that in which the active intelligence shows itself operating within a limited circuit, as in a single mind. This is the principle of individuality; not as though the infinite intelligence were something different from the finite, or as though there were an infinite intelligence out of and apart from the finite, but it is merely the absolute in one of its particular moments; just as an individual thought is but a single moment of the whole mind. Each finite reason, then, is but a thought of the infinite and eternal reason." The absolute essence being thus everything, all difference between God and the universe is truly lost; and Pantheism becomes complete, "as the absolute is evolved from its lowest form to the highest, in accordance with the necessary law or rhythm of its being, the whole world, material and mental, becoming one enormous chain of necessity, to which no idea of free creation can be attached." * Again : " Deity is a process ever going on, but never accomplished; nay, the Divine consciousness is absolutely one with the advancing consciousness of mankind. The hope of immortality perishes; for death is but the return of the individual to the infinite, and man is annihilated, though the Deity will eternally live." † Once more : " Deity is the eternal process of self-development as realised *in man;* the Divine and human consciousness falling absolutely together." "The knowledge of God and of his manifestations forms the subject of speculative theology. . . . Of these manifestations there are three great spheres of observation—nature, mind, and humanity. In nature we see the Divine idea in its lowest expression; in mind, with its powers, faculties, moral feelings, freedom, &c., we see it in its higher and more perfect form; lastly, in humanity we see God, not only as creator and sustainer, but also as a father and a guide." " The soul is a perfect mirror of the universe; and we have only to gaze into it with earnest attention to discover all truth which

---

* See account of the German school, Schelling, Hegel, and Hillebrand, in Morell's History of Modern Philosophy, vol. ii. pp. 126-147.

† Ibid. p. 196.

is accessible to humanity. What we know of God, therefore, can be only that which is originally revealed to us of Him in our own minds."* I have given these extracts to show the legitimate resolution of the subjective system of private judgment into pure rationalistic Pantheism.

With a few words on the Positivism of Comte, I will conclude. Lest I should appear to distort or colour this form of aberration, I will give it in the author's own words.

First, then, he describes the Positive philosophy as follows:

"From the study of the development of human intelligence, in all directions and through all times, the discovery arises of a great fundamental law, to which it is necessarily subject, and which has a solid foundation of proof, both in the facts of our organisation and in our historical experience. The law is this: that each of our leading conceptions, each branch of our knowledge, passes successively through three different theoretical conditions—the Theological or fictitious; the Metaphysical or abstract; and the Scientific or positive. In other words, the human mind by its nature employs in its progress three methods of philosophising, the character of which is essentially different and even radically opposed, viz. the theological method, the metaphysical, and the

* Morell's History of Modern Philosophy, vol. ii. p. 225.

positive. Hence arise three philosophies, or general systems of conceptions, on the aggregate of phenomena, each of which excludes the others. The first is the necessary point of departure of the human understanding, and the third is its fixed and definite state. The second is merely a state of transition.

"In the theological state, the human mind, seeking the essential nature of beings, the first and final causes (the origin and purpose) of all effects,—in short, absolute knowledge,—supposes all phenomena to be produced by the immediate action of supernatural beings.

"In the metaphysical state, which is only a modification of the first, the mind supposes, instead of supernatural beings, abstract forces, veritable entities (that is, personified abstractions), inherent in all beings, and capable of producing all phenomena. What is called the explanation of phenomena is, in this stage, a mere reference of each to its proper entity.

"In the final, the positive state, the mind has given over the search after absolute notions, the origin and destination of the universe, and the causes of phenomena, and applies itself to the study of their laws, that is, their invariable relations of succession and resemblance. Reasoning and observation, duly combined, are the means of this knowledge. What is now understood, when we speak of an explanation of facts, is simply the establishment of a connexion between single phenomena and some general facts, the number of which continually diminishes with the progress of science." *

From this it will be observed that the belief in God has passed into the first or fictitious period of the human reason.

Nevertheless, after the completion of his *Philosophy*, Comte perceived the necessity of a religion. Hence the *Catechism of Positive Religion*, which thus begins: "In the name of the Past and of the Future, the servants of Humanity—both its philosophical and practical servants—come forward to claim as their due the general direction of this world. Their object is, to constitute at length a real Providence in all departments, moral, intellectual, and material. Consequently they exclude, once for all, from political supremacy all the different servants of God—Catholic, Protestant, or Deist—as being at once behindhand and a cause of disturbance." †

But inasmuch as there can be no religion without worship, and no worship without a God, and inasmuch as there is no God, Comte had need to find or to create a Divinity. Now as there is no God, there can be no being higher than man, and no object of worship higher than mankind. "The imaginary

---

* Positive Philosophy, vol. i. c. 1.
† Catechism of Positive Religion, Preface.

beings whom religion provisionally introduced for its purposes were able to inspire lively affections in man —affections which were even most powerful under the least elaborate of the fictitious systems. The immense scientific preparation required as an introduction to Positivism for a long time seemed to deprive it of any such valuable aptitude. Whilst the philosophical initiation only comprehended the order of the material world, nay, even when it had extended to the order of living beings, it could only reveal laws which were indispensable for our action ; it could not furnish us with any direct object for an enduring and constant affection. This is no longer the case since the completion of our gradual preparation by the introduction of the special study of the order of man's existence, whether as an individual or as a society. This is the last step in the process. We are now able to condense the whole of our Positive conceptions in the one single idea of an immense and eternal Being, Humanity, destined by sociological laws to constant development under the preponderating influence of biological and cosmological necessities. This the real great Being, on whom all, whether individuals or societies, depend as the prime mover of their existence, becomes the centre of our affections. They rest on it by as spontaneous an impulse as do our thoughts and our actions. This Being, by its very idea, suggests at once the sacred formula of Positivism;—*Love as our principle, Order as our basis, and Progress as our end.* Its compound existence is ever founded on the free concurrence of independent wills. All discord tends to dissolve that existence, which, by its very notion, sanctions the constant predominance of the heart over the intellect, as the sole basis of our true unity. So the whole order of things henceforth finds its expression in the being who studies it, and who is ever perfecting it. The struggle of Humanity against the combined influences of the necessities it is obliged to obey, growing as it does in energy and success, offers the heart, no less than the intellect, a better object of contemplation than the capricious omnipotence of its theological precursor—capricious by the very force of the word omnipotence. Such a Supreme Being is more within the reach of our feelings as well as of our conceptions, for it is identical in nature with its servants, at the same time that it is superior to them."

"You must define Humanity as *the whole* of human beings, past, present, and future. The word *whole* points out clearly that you must not take in all men, but those only who are really capable of assimilation, in virtue of a real co-operation on their part in furthering the common good. All are necessarily born children of Humanity, but all do not become her servants. Many remain in the parasitic state, which, excusable during their education, becomes blamable when that education is complete. Times of anarchy bring forth in swarms such creatures, nay, even enable them to flourish, though they are, in sad truth, but burdens on the true Great Being." *

It will be observed that both Pantheism and Positivism alike end in the deification of man; they are a boundless egotism and an apotheosis of human pride. I shall not dwell further on this point; and mention it only because I shall have to refer to it hereafter.

I will now briefly sum up what I have said.

We see that it is foretold, that, before the manifestation of the last great antagonist of God and of His incarnate Son, there must be a revolt and falling away; we have seen that the authority from which the revolt is to be made is manifestly that of the Church of God, and that it will be a revolt bearing the three notes of schism, heresy, and denial of the Incarnation; we see also that this Antichristian movement was at work even in the days of the Apostles; that it has wrought ever since in manifold forms and various times, and with most diverse, and even contradictory, developments, but that nevertheless it is always one and the same, identical in principle and in antagonism to the Incarnation and to the Church. It is evident that this movement has accumulated its results from age to age, and that

* Catechism of Positive Religion, pp. 63, 74.

at this time it is more mature and has a loftier stature and a greater power and a more formal antagonism to the Church and the faith than ever before.

It has attached itself to the pride of governments by nationalism, and of individuals by philosophy, and, under the forms of Protestantism, Civilisation, Secularism, it has organised a vast Anticatholic power in the east, north, and west of Europe. As a matter of fact, Catholic and Anticatholic describe the two arrays. I am afraid I must add, Christian and Antichristian. And this is one of my purposes in treating of the subject before us; for I am convinced that multitudes are carried away, not knowing whither they go, by a movement essentially opposed to all their best and deepest convictions, because they are unable to discern its real ultimate principle and character.

In the present array of the popular opinion of Europe against the Holy See and the Vicar of Jesus Christ, may be discerned the Antichristian instinct. The revolutions in Italy, backed by the Anticatholic spirit of the Continent, and by the policy of England, are fulfilling the prophecies, and confirming our faith. But this I shall hope to show more fully hereafter. It seems inevitable that the enmity of all nations which are separated from the Catholic unity, and penetrated by the spirit of the Reformation, that is, by the spirit of private judgment as opposed to the Divine Voice of the living

Church, and by the unbelief which has banished the Eucharistical presence of the Incarnate Word, should be concentrated upon the person who is the Vicar and Representative of Jesus, and upon the Body which witnesses alone for the Incarnation, and for all its mysteries of truth and grace. Such is the one Holy Catholic and Roman Church, and such is the Supreme Pontiff, its Visible Head. Such, in the words of Holy Scripture, are the two mysteries of godliness and of iniquity. All things are throwing out into light and prominence the two ultimate powers which divide the destinies of men. The conflict is a simple antagonism of Christ and Antichrist; and the two arrays are marshalling in order, and men are choosing their principles; or events are choosing for them, and they are drifting unconsciously into currents, of which they are not aware. The theory, that politics and religion have different spheres, is an illusion and a snare. For history can only be truly read in the light of faith; and the present can only be interpreted by the light of revelation: for above the human wills which are now in conflict, there is a Will, sovereign and divine, which is leading all things to fulfil its own perfect end.

LECTURE II.

SUCH, then, is the Revolt, which has been gathering strength these 1800 years, and ripening for the hour when it shall receive its leader and head.

The interpretation universally received by Anti-catholic controversialists, whereby, first, Antichrist is held to be a spirit or system, and not a person, and next, to be the Catholic or Roman Church, or the Vicar of the Incarnate Word, is the master-stroke of deceit. It allays all fear, and inspires presumption and confidence, and fixes the attention of men to watch for the signs of his appearing anywhere except where they are to be seen; and draws it off from the quarter where they are already visible.

Now, I do not hesitate to say, that, in all the prophecies of Revelation, there is not one among them which relates to the coming of Christ more explicit and express than those which relate to the coming of Antichrist.

1. He is described with all the attributes of a person. In this one passage St. Paul calls him "that wicked one," ὁ ἄνομος, *ille iniquus;* the "man of sin," ἄνθρωπος τῆς ἁμαρτίας, *homo peccati;* and "son of

perdition," υἱὸς τῆς ἀπωλείας. And St. John in four places speaks of him as the Antichrist. To deny the personality of Antichrist, is therefore to deny the plain testimony of Holy Scripture: to explain away these personal terms and titles as of a system or spirit, is as rationalistic as the impiety of Strauss in denying "the historical," that is, the personal Christ.

It is a law of Holy Scripture, that when persons are prophesied of, persons appear; as, for instance, the prophecies of St. John Baptist, or of the Blessed Virgin, or of our Lord Himself.

All the Fathers, both of the East and West,—St. Irenæus, St. Cyprian, St. Jerome, St. Ambrose, St. Cyril of Jerusalem, St. Gregory of Nazianzum, St. John Chrysostom, Theophylact, Ecumenius,—all interpret these passages of a literal and personal Antichrist. What I may call the corporate interpretation is modern, heretical, controversial, and unreasonable. This fanciful and contradictory system has been sufficiently destroyed even by Protestant writers: as by Todd in his work on Antichrist, a creditable and learned book, though somewhat defaced by the *reliquiæ* of Protestant prejudice; by Greswell, in his *Exposition of the Parables;* and by Maitland on Daniel and St. John. In Germany, even among Protestant interpreters, to maintain the Anticatholic interpretation is looked on as a surrender of the character of a biblical scholar. The Protestants of England are still, as they always were, the least cultivated and reasonable. It is true, indeed, that the Antichrist has had, and may still have, many forerunners as had also Christ Himself: as Isaac, Moses, Josue, David, Jeremias, were types of the one, so Antiochus, Julian, Arius, Mahomet, and many more, are the types of the other; for persons typify persons. So, again, as Christ is the Head and Representative in which the whole mystery of godliness (τὸ τῆς εὐσεβείας μυστήριον *) has been summed up and recapitulated, so also the whole mystery of impiety (τὸ μυστήριον τῆς ἀνομίας †) will find its expression and its head in the person of Antichrist. He may indeed embody a spirit and represent a system, but is not less, therefore, a person. So also the theologians. Bellarmine says, "All Catholics hold that Antichrist will be one individual person." ‡ Lessius says, "All agree in teaching that the proper Antichrist will be not many, but one only person." § Suarez goes so far as to say that this doctrine of the personal Antichrist of faith is "certain *de fide*." ||

2. Next, the Fathers believed that Antichrist will be of the Jewish race. Such was the opinion of St. Irenæus, St. Jerome, of the author of the work *De*

---

* 1 Tim. iii. 16.   † 2 Thess. ii. 7.
† Bellarm. de Summo Pontif. lib. iii. c. 2.
§ De Antichristo, Tertia Dem.
|| In iii. p. D. Thomæ, Disp. liv. s. 1.

Consummatione Mundi ascribed to St. Hippolytus, of the writer of a commentary on the Epistle to the Thessalonians attributed to St. Ambrose, and of many others, who add that he will be of the tribe of Dan; as, for instance, St. Gregory the Great, Theodoret, Aretas of Cæsarea, and many more.* Such also is the opinion of Bellarmine, who calls it certain.† Lessius affirms that the Fathers, with unanimous consent, teach as undoubted that Antichrist will be a Jew.‡ Ribera repeats the same opinion, and adds that Aretas, St. Bede, Haymo, St. Anselm, and Rupert affirm that for this reason the tribe of Dan is not numbered among those who are sealed in the Apocalypse.§ Viegas says the same, quoting other authorities.|| And this will appear probable, if we consider that the Antichrist will come to deceive the Jews, according to the prophecy of our Lord: "I am come in My Father's name, and you receive Me not: another will come in his own name, him you will receive;" which words are interpreted by the Fathers with one consent of the false Messias, who shall pass himself off upon the Jews as the true. And this, again, is the unanimous interpretation of the Fathers both of the East and of the West, as St. Cyril of Jerusalem, St. Ephraim Syrus, St. Gregory

---

* Malvenda de Antichristo, lib. ii. cc. x. xi.
† Ibid. c. xii. ‡ Ibid. in præfatione.
§ Ribera, in Apoc. c. vii. || Viegas, in Apoc. c. vii.

Nazianzen, St. Gregory Nyssen, St. John Damascene, and also of St. Irenæus, St. Cyprian, St. Jerome, St. Ambrose, and St. Augustine. The probability of this also will appear, if we consider, further, that a false Christ would fail of the first condition of success if he were not of the house of David; that the Jews are still looking out for his coming; that they have prepared themselves for delusion by crucifying the true Messias; and therefore it is that the Fathers interpret of the true Messias and the false the words of St. Paul to the Thessalonians: "Because they received not the love of the truth (τὴν ἀγάπην τῆς ἀληθείας) that they might be saved; therefore God shall send them the operation of error (ἐνέργειαν πλάνης) to believe lying."*

Now, I think no one can consider the dispersion and providential preservation of the Jews among all nations of the world, the indestructible vitality of their race, without believing that they are reserved for some future action of His judgment and grace. And this is foretold again and again in the New Testament; for instance, in the Epistles to the Romans and the Corinthians.†

3. From this we perceive a third character of Antichrist, namely, that he will not be simply the antagonist, but the substitute or supplanter of the true

---

* 2 Thess. ii. 10, 11.
† Rom. xi. 15-24; 2 Cor. iii. 16.

Messias.* And this is rendered still more probable by the fact, that the Messias looked for by the Jews has always been a temporal deliverer, the restorer of their temporal power; or, in other words, a political and military prince. It is obvious also, that whosoever may hereafter deceive them in the pretended character of their Messias, must thereby deny the Incarnation, whatsoever claim to a supernatural character he may put forward for himself. In his own person he will be a complete denial of the whole Christian faith and Church; for if he be the true Messias, the Christ of the Christians must be false.

Now, perhaps, we do not sufficiently realise how commonplace and historical a person such a deceiver may be. We are so possessed with the idea and vision of the true Messias in the glory of His Godhead and Manhood, of His Divine actions and Passion, of His Resurrection, Ascension, and royalties over the world and the Church, that we cannot conceive how any false Christ could be received as the true. It is for this reason that our Lord has said of these latter times: "There shall arise false Christs and false prophets, insomuch as to deceive (if possible) even the elect;" † that is, they shall not be

---

* Suarez, ut supra, Disp. liv. s. 4; Lessius, Dem. vii. 21; Bellarm. ibid. c. xiv. s. 13. See also Gresswell on the Parables, vol. i. 371, note n.

† St. Matt. xxiv. 24.

deceived; but those who have lost faith in the Incarnation, such as Humanitarians, Rationalists, and Pantheists, may well be deceived by any person of great political power and success who should restore the Jews to their own land, and people Jerusalem once more with the sons of the patriarchs. And there is nothing in the political aspect of the world which renders such a combination impossible; indeed, the state of Syria, and the tide of European diplomacy which is continually moving eastward, render such an event within a reasonable probability.

4. But the prophecies assign to the person of Antichrist a more preternatural character.* He is described as a worker of false miracles. His coming is said to be "according to the working of Satan, in all power, and signs, and lying wonders, and in all seduction of iniquity to them that perish."†

And here I cannot but perceive a wonderful change which has passed upon the world. Half a century ago the men who rejected Christianity derided a belief in witchcraft as superstition, and in miracles as foolishness. But now the world has outstripped even the faith of Christians by its credulity. Europe and America are deluged by Spiritualism. I know not how many hundreds and thousands of

---

* Bellarm. ibid. c. xv. ; Lessius, ibid. x. 34 ; De Præcursoribus Antichristi, x. 37.
† 2 Thess. ii 9, 10.

mediums between us and the unseen world are in existence. The very men who would not permit the witch of Endor, or Elymas the sorcerer, to pass without ridicule, believe in table-turning and table-rapping, in clairvoyance, and the communications of spirits evoked from the world unseen; in spirit-writing, and locomotion through the air, and in the apparition of hands, and even of persons. Revelation of the state of the dead, of secrets among the living, prolonged and repeated colloquies with the departed, are not only believed, but practised habitually, and almost day by day. Now, it is not my object, at least not now, to appreciate these phenomena. It is enough for us to say, that to us who believe in an unseen world, and in the presence and warfare of spirits, good and evil, such things present no difficulty. We are not disposed to deny their reality because of the falsehood or delusion which is mixed up with them. They are precisely what the Church has always condemned and forbidden under the name of witchcraft: in which there is a real preternatural agency surrounded by much imposture. I dwell on this point because it is certain that we are encompassed by a supernatural order, of which part is divine, and part is diabolical. It is not wonderful that they who reject the divine supernatural order should become immoderately credulous of the diabolical. Now in this we have already a preparation for the deception of which St. Paul writes. The age is ripe for a delusion. It will not believe the miracles of the saints, but it will copiously drink down the phenomena of spiritualism. A successful medium might well pass himself off by his preternatural endowments as the promised Messias, and "signs and lying wonders" in abundance may be wrought by the agencies which are already abroad in the world.

5. The last characteristic of which I will speak is more difficult, perhaps, to conceive. St. Paul says of "the man of sin," "the son of perdition, who opposeth and is lifted up above all that is called God or that is worshipped; so that he sitteth in the temple of God, showing himself as if he were God." * These words are interpreted by the Fathers to mean that he will claim divine honours, and that in the Temple of Jerusalem. St. Irenæus says that "Antichrist being an apostate and a robber, will claim to be adored as God," and "that he will endeavour to show himself off as God."† Lactantius, that "he will call himself God." ‡ The writer under the name of St. Ambrose, says, "He will affirm himself to be God." St. Jerome, "He will call himself God, and claim to be worshipped by all."§ St. John Chryso-

---

* 2 Thess. ii. 4.   † St. Iren. lib. v. 29.
‡ Lactantius, de divinis Institutionibus, lib. vii. c. 17.
§ St. Hieron. in Zach. c. xi.

stom, " He will profess himself to be the God of all, and call himself and show himself off as God."* So also Theodoret, Theophylact, Ecumenius, St. Anselm, and many others.†

Suarez, in explaining this passage, says, "It is likely that Antichrist will in no way believe himself what he will teach and compel others to believe. For though in the beginning he may persuade the Jews that he is the Messias and is sent from God, and may pretend to believe that the law of Moses is true and to be observed, yet he will do all this in dissimulation, to deceive them and to obtain supreme power. For afterwards he will reject the law of Moses, and will deny the true God who gave it. For which reason many believe that he will craftily destroy idolatry in order to deceive the Jews." "How great his perfidy will be, and what he will really believe concerning God, we cannot conjecture. But it is likely that he will be an atheist, and will deny both reward and punishment in another life, and will venerate only the preternatural being, from whom he has learned the art of deceit and acquired his riches, by which wealth he will obtain supreme power."‡

Now, it is easy to understand how he will oppose God, being the antagonist of Christ; and how he

---

* St. Joan. Chrys. in St. Joan. Hom. xl.
† Malvenda, lib. vii. c. 4.
‡ Suarez, in iii. p. St. Thomæ, Disp. liv. s. 4.

will exalt or lift himself above all that is called God and worshipped; because, in supplanting the true Messias, he places himself in the stead of the Incarnate God. Nor is it difficult to understand how those who have lost the true and divine idea of the Messias may accept a false; and, being dazzled by the greatness of political and military successes,* and inflated with the Pantheistic and Socinian notions of the dignity of man, may pay to the person of Antichrist the honour which Christians pay to the true Messias. I have touched on this because St. Paul places it prominently in the description of Antichrist, and because the tendency of the credulous unbelief, which increases in the world as faith decreases, is visibly preparing men for delusion.

It is one of the most wonderful interpretations of the Fathers, that in the end of the world paganism shall be restored.† This at least we should have thought impossible: if for no other reason, at least from the development of modern infidelity; and yet infidelity was never more dominant than when in the first French Revolution Christianity was voted to be false, and the worship of Reason and Ceres set up in its place. In truth, when the intellectual become Pantheists, the simple will become Polytheists. They need a more material conception than the refined

---

* St. Aug. in Psalm ix. tom. iv. 54.
† Cornelius à Lapide in Apocal. c. xvii.

unbelievers, and they impersonate and embody, first in thought and then in form, the object of their worship. And what is this but paganism simple and pure? But into this I cannot enter. In the second *livraison* of Gaume's work on the French Revolution, especially in the 12th, 13th, and 14th chapters, will be found an ample and detailed account of the paganism of fifty years ago; and in the *Catechism of Positive Religion*, under the head of "Public and Private Worship," will be seen an elaborate profession of religious worship addressed to humanity—the collective body of deified men, which is the natural basis of the religion of ancient Greece and Rome.

Now, I do not say that there may not be far more stupendous and preternatural phenomena about the manifestation and person of Antichrist. All history would lead us to expect it; all the prophecies seem to predict it; the great periods of divine action in the world foreshadow it. My object has not been to divest the future of the supernatural, but to show how the supernatural mingles itself in the ordinary course of the world, and steals upon us, so to speak, unawares. "The kingdom of God cometh not with observation," but is in the midst of us, in full presence and power, under aspects which seem to us common and unmarked, in the currents of human action, in national movements, in the policy of governments, and the diplomacy of the world. As Christ at His coming was believed to be the Carpenter, so Antichrist may be visibly no more than a successful adventurer. Even his preternatural character, true or false, may pass either as scintillations of insanity, or as the absurdities of his partisans, or the delusions of his flatterers. So the world blinds its own eyes by the fumes of its own intellectual pride. There is nothing out of the context or proportion, or $ἦθος$, as we are wont to say of the nineteenth century, that a person should arise of Jewish blood, naturalised in some of the peoples of Europe, a protector of the Jews, the purse-bearers, and journalists, and telegraphic wires, of the revolutions of Europe, hailed by them as their saviour from the social and political dominion of the Christians, surrounded by the phenomena of antichristian and anticatholic spiritualism, an arch-medium himself, and professing to be more than either Moses or Mahomet, that is, more than of human stature and proportions.

To those who have never discerned the ultimate unity in principle and action of truth, on the one side, and of falsehood, on the other, and likewise respectively of good and evil, it may appear strange to attach much importance to any event the sphere of which seems to be the Jewish race. But to those who believe that the world may be divided into Christian and Antichristian, or Catholic and Anticatholic,—or, in other words, into the natural order, based upon the mere human will and action, and the supernatural, based on the Divine will and the Incarnation of God,—it will at once be seen to be the question most vital and decisive of all. I shall hope to show hereafter that the antagonism between two persons is an antagonism also between two societies, and that as our Divine Lord is the Head and Representative of all the truth and justice of the world from the beginning, so Antichrist, be he who or what he may, will be the head and representative of all the falsehood and wrong, which has been accumulating for these 1800 years, in the heresies, schisms, spiritual seditions, intellectual infidelities, social disorders, and political revolutions of the anticatholic movements of the world.

Such is the great deep upon which the Christian society of the world is resting. From time to time it has lifted itself up with a preternatural power, and has made the Christian order of Europe vibrate and reel. Then again it has seemed to subside into a calm. But no one with any discernment can fail to see that it is deeper, mightier, and more widely spread now than ever. That this antichristian power will one day find its head, and for a time prevail in this world, is certain from prophecy. But this cannot be until " he who holdeth " shall be taken out of the way. This, however, is the next subject in our order, and I must not anticipate it here.

LECTURE III.

Before I enter on our third subject, let us call to mind the two points, which, I hope, have been established in what I have hitherto said. The first is, that we see the revolt, or falling away, already verified and manifested in the spiritual separations from the Church, and in the opposition to its Divine authority and its Divine voice, which we traced in history from the day when the Apostle said, " The mystery of iniquity doth already work," and St. John declared that the Antichrists were already gone out into the world. The other point we have seen is this, that the man of sin, the son of perdition—the wicked one—is a person, in all probability, of the Jewish race; that he is to be a supplanter of the true Messias, and therefore an Antichrist in the sense of substituting himself in the place of the true,—a worker of false miracles, and claiming for himself Divine worship.

Now the third point on which I have to speak is the hindrance which retards his manifestation. The Apostle says, " The mystery of iniquity doth already work; only that he who now holdeth " (that is, stands in the way of the revelation of the man of sin) " hold until" (the time that) "he be taken out of the way." As there is a perpetual working of this mystery of iniquity, so there is a perpetual hindrance or barrier to its full manifestation, which will continue until it be removed; and there is a fixed time when it shall be taken out of the way. St. Paul, in this passage, uses two expressions. He says, the hindrance "*which* holdeth," and "*who* holdeth." He speaks of it as of a thing and as of a person : τὸ κατέχον and ὁ κατέχων. At first sight there appears to be a difficulty, whether that which hinders the revelation of the man of sin be a person or a system ; for in the one place it is spoken of in the neuter as a system, in the other case it is spoken of in the masculine as a person. I hope in what I have hitherto said that I have already given a solution to this apparent difficulty. You will remember that I drew out shortly the parallel of the two mysteries of godliness and of iniquity, and of their respective heads. This is, in fact, the argument of St. Augustine, who has sketched the two mysteries of godliness and of iniquity, from the beginning of the world, under the character of the two cities—that is, the Spirit of God and the spirit of Satan, working by a manifold operation either in the elect servants of God, or in the enemies of God and of His Kingdom. And just as the mystery of godliness is summed up in the person and Incarnation of the Son of God, so the mystery of iniquity is summed up in the man of sin, who shall be revealed in his time. In like manner also, that which hinders, or he who hinders, will be found to express both a system and a person, and the person and the system to be identified after the same manner as the examples which I have already given.

First of all, let us consider more particularly what is the character of "this wicked one," or Antichrist, who shall come. The word used by St. Paul in this place signifies "the lawless one,"—the one who is without law, who is not subject to the law of God or of man, whose only law is his own will, to whom the licence of his own will is the sole and only rule which he knows or obeys. The Greek word is ὁ ἄνομος, the lawless, or licentious one. Now, in the book of the prophet Daniel, there is a prophecy, almost identical in terms, where he foretells that there shall arise in the latter ages of the world a king "who shall do according to his own will," * who shall exalt himself above all that is called God, who "shall speak great words against the High one." † This is almost word for word the prophecy of St. Paul, which shows us that St. Paul was literally quoting or paraphrasing the prophecy of Daniel. Now, inasmuch as this wicked one shall be a lawless person, who shall introduce disorder, sedition, tumult, and revolution,

* Or "pleasure," Dan. xi. 16.   † Dan. vii. 25.

both in the temporal and spiritual order of the world, so that which shall hinder his development, and shall be his direct antagonist after his manifestation, must necessarily be the principle of order, the law of submission, the authority of truth and of right. We therefore have got what I may call an indication to enable us to see where this person, or system which opposes, hinders, or holds the revelation of the man of sin until the season shall come, is to be found.

Let us, then, examine the interpretations of the early Fathers on this point.

Tertullian * believed that it was the Roman Empire. The mighty power of Pagan Rome, spread throughout the whole world, was the great principle of order which maintained at that time the tranquillity of the earth.

Lactantius,† who wrote later, maintained exactly the same opinion, and believed that the Roman Empire, which tranquillised and gave order and peace to the nations of the world, thereby hindered the revelation of this lawless one—this man of sin; and both Tertullian and Lactantius enjoined upon the Christians of their time the duty of praying for the preservation of the heathen empire of Rome, because they believed it to be the material barrier against the breaking-in of the great flood of evil which should

---

* Tertull. de Resur. Carnis, c. 24.
† Divin. Inst. vii. 25.

come upon the world when Rome is destroyed. So also teach St. John Chrysostom and others.*

Another interpretation, which is given by Theodoret, a Greek writer, is, that it is the grace of the Holy Ghost, or the Divine power, which restrains the manifestation or the revelation of the man of sin.†

Again, other writers say that it is the apostolic power, or the presence of the Apostles; for, as we know from this epistle to the Thessalonians, the Christians were expecting a speedy revelation of the coming of our Lord to judgment, and therefore a speedy manifestation of the man of sin; and they believed that the presence of the Apostles upon earth, by their witness and by their miracles, hindered the full manifestation of the principle of unbelief and spiritual of rebellion.

Now these three interpretations are all of them partially true, and all are in perfect harmony one with the other; and we shall find that, taken together, they present us with a full and adequate explanation; but these writers, writing at different periods of the Church, were not able fully to understand the prophecy, because the events of the world are continually and progressively interpreting and explaining, from age to age, the meaning of these predictions.

1. First, then, the power of the heathen empire of

---

* Malvenda, lib. ii. c. 3.
† Theodor. in 2 Ep. ad Thess. c. ii. 6.

Rome was undoubtedly the great barrier against the outbreak of the spirit of lawless disorder; for, as we know, it was the principle of unity by which the nations of the world were held together. It organised and combined them under the authority of one legislature, of one mighty executive, and of one great sovereignty, with a jurisdiction springing from one fountain, administered by tribunals all over the world. The peace of nations was maintained by the presence of standing armies; the legions of Rome occupied the circumference of the world. The military roads which sprang from Rome traversed all the earth; the whole world was as it were held in peace and in tranquillity by the universal presence of this mighty heathen empire. It was "exceedingly terrible," * according to the prophecies of Daniel; it was as it were of iron, beating down and subduing the nations, holding them in subjugation, and thereby, as with a rod of iron, giving peace to the world. There is no doubt that so long as the Roman Empire continued in its strength, it was impossible for the principle of revolution and disorder to gain head, and therefore these early Christian writers were perfectly correct in interpreting the hindrance to this spirit of lawlessness to be the spirit of order, of government, of authority, and of an iron justice, which ruled the nations of the world.

* Dan. vii. 19.

2. But, secondly, it was not the Roman Empire, or Rome alone, but the kingdom of God which descended upon the whole earth, and from the day of Pentecost spread throughout the circuit of the Roman Empire, with an authority higher than the authority of Rome. St. Leo gives the basis of this interpretation.* He says, "That the effect of this ineffable grace might be diffused throughout the world, He (God) prepared the empire of Rome, the expansion of which was extended to the limits which border upon the whole family of all nations. For it was a fitting preparation for the work divinely disposed that many kingdoms should be confederated in one empire, so that the universal preaching of the Gospel should penetrate speedily through those nations whom the government of one city held in unity." St. Thomas, resting upon this passage, says that the Roman Empire has not ceased, but is changed from the temporal into the spiritual, *commutatum de temporali in spiritale*.† Dominicus Soto holds the same opinion.‡ It was, then, the Apostolic Church which, spreading throughout all the nations, already combined together by the power of the heathen empire of Rome, quickened them with a new life, penetrated them with a new principle of order, with a new spirit of unity,

---

* St. Leo, Serm. lxxxii. t. i. p. 322.
† In 2 Ep. ad Thess. in locum.
‡ In lib. lv. Sent. Distinc. xlvi. 1.

consecrated and transfigured the unity of the material forces by which they were held together, gave them one mind, one intelligence, one law, one will, one heart, by the faith which illuminated the intelligence of all nations to know God, by the charity which bound them together in the unity of one family, by the one fountain of jurisdiction which sprang from our Divine Lord, and through His Apostles governed the whole earth. There was the one spiritual legislature of the Apostles and their successors. There were tribunals which sat beside the tribunals of Rome. By the side of the tribunals of iron force were erected the tribunals of Divine mercy. This new principle of order, of authority, of submission, and of peace, entered into this world, possessed itself, as I may say, of the material power of the old Roman Empire, and filled it with a new life from heaven. It was the salt of the earth. It prolonged its existence until a certain period, which was foreseen in the predestination of God. It is, therefore, perfectly true that this hindrance signifies also the Holy Ghost; for the Church of God is the presence of the Holy Ghost, incorporated and manifested to the world in the visible body of those who are baptized into the unity of the Church of Jesus Christ.

3. But then, thirdly, it means something still more than this. For these two great powers, spiritual and temporal—the temporal power in the old heathen

empire of Rome, and the spiritual power in the new supernatural kingdom of God—met together. They were coincident as it were in their circumference throughout the world; but they met together in their centre, which was in the city of Rome. There they stood, at first face to face in conflict, then side by side in peace. There these two mighty powers—the one from earth, and the other from heaven, the one from the will of man, and the other from the will of God—met together as it were in the arena of contest, and for three hundred years the Empire of Rome martyred the pontiffs of the Church of God. For three hundred years the Roman Empire strove to extinguish this new and strange visitant, coming with a superior jurisdiction and with a wider circuit. It strove to destroy it, to quench it in its own blood; and for three hundred years it struggled in vain; for the more the Church was martyred, the more the seed of the martyrs was multiplied. The Church expanded and grew in vigour, in strength, and in power, in proportion as the heathen Empire of Rome strove to extinguish it and to destroy it. And this mighty conflict between the two sovereignties at last ended in the conversion of the Empire to Christianity, and, therefore, in the enthronement of the Church of God in a supremacy over the powers of the whole world. Then right had power and supremacy over might, and the Divine authority prevailed over the authority of man; then these two powers were blended and fused together: they became one great authority, the emperor ruling from his throne within the sphere of his earthly jurisdiction, and the Supreme Pontiff ruling likewise from a throne of higher sovereignty over the nations of the world, until God in His providence removed the empire from Rome, and planted it upon the shores of the Bosphorus. It departed into the East, and left Rome without a sovereign. Rome from that hour has never had, dwelling within its walls, a temporal sovereign in the presence of the Supreme Pontiff; and that temporal sovereignty devolved by a providential law upon the person of the Vicar of Jesus Christ. It is true, indeed, that in the three centuries between the conversion of Constantine and the period of St. Gregory the Great, in those three centuries of turbulence and disorder, invasion and warfare, by which Italy and Rome was afflicted, the temporal power of the Supreme Pontiff was only in its beginning; but about the seventh century it was firmly established, and that which the Divine Providence had prepared from the beginning received its full manifestation; and no sooner was the material power which once reigned in Rome consecrated and sanctified by the investiture of the Vicar of Jesus Christ with temporal sovereignty over the city where he dwelt, than he began to create throughout Europe the order of Christian civilisation,

Christian empires, Christian monarchies, which, confederated together, have maintained the peace and order of the world from that hour to this. What we call Christendom, that is to say, the great family of Christian nations, Christian races organised and knit together with their princes and their legislatures, by international law, mutual contracts, treaties, diplomacy, and the like, which bind them together in one compact body,—what is this but the security of the world against disorder, turbulence, and lawlessness? And now for these twelve hundred years the peace, the perpetuity, and the fruitfulness of the Christian civilisation of Europe, has been owing solely in its principle to this consecration of the power and the authority of the great Empire of Rome, taken up of old, perpetuated, preserved, as I have said, by the salt which had been sprinkled from heaven and continued in the person of the Supreme Pontiff, and in that order of Christian civilisation of which he has been the creator.

We have now come nearly to a solution of that which I stated in the beginning, namely, how it is that the power which hinders the revelation of the lawless one is not only a person but a system, and not only a system but a person. In one word, it is Christendom and its head; and, therefore, in the person of the Vicar of Jesus Christ, and in that twofold authority with which, by Divine Providence, he has been invested, we see the direct antagonist to the principle of disorder. The lawless one, who knows no law, human or divine, nor obeys any but his own will, has no antagonist on earth more direct than the Vicar of Jesus Christ, who bears at one and the same time the character of royalty and of priesthood, and represents the two principles of order in the temporal and in the spiritual state—the principle of monarchy, if you will, or of government, and the principle of the apostolic authority. We find, therefore, the three interpretations which I drew out from the Holy Fathers literally verified in this. In the slow course of time, as the work of the Apostles matured and ripened, what we call Christendom has arisen, fulfilling the predictions to the letter, manifesting that which the Apostle foretold would hinder the development of this principle of lawlessness, and the revelation of the person who should be its chief.

What, then, is it that at this moment holds in check the manifestation of this antichristian power, and the person who shall wield it? It is the remnant of the Christian society which is still existing in the world. There can be but two societies, the one natural, the other supernatural. The natural society is the political order which comes from the will of man, without relation to the revelation, or the Incarnation of God. The supernatural society is the Church, comprehending those nations which still, being penetrated by the spirit of faith and of the Catholic unity, are true and faithful to the principles upon which Christendom was first constituted.

Ever since the foundation of Christian Europe, the political order of the world has rested upon the Incarnation of our Lord Jesus Christ; for which reason all the public acts of authority, and even the calendar by which we date our days, is calculated from the year of salvation, or from "the year of our Lord." What is the meaning of this phrase, if it be not this, that the state and order under which we live is based upon the Incarnation; that Christianity is our foundation; that we recognise the revealed laws of God delivered to His incarnate Son, and by the incarnate Son to the Apostles, and by the Apostles to the world, as the first principles of all Christian legislation and of all Christian society? Now this society based upon the Incarnation is the state under which we have hitherto lived. I believe that we are departing from it. We are departing from it throughout the whole of the civilised world. In England, religion is banished from politics. In many countries, such as France, and now in Austria, it is declared by public act that the State has no religion, that all sects are equally participators in the political life and political power of the nation. Now a large portion of every nation, a large portion especially of France and of Austria, is composed of that race who deny the coming of God

I

in the flesh, that is, who deny the Incarnation. I am not now arguing against their admission to political privileges; on the contrary, I would maintain, that, if there be no other order than the order of nature, it would be a political injustice to exclude any one of the race of Israel from a participation of equal privileges; but I maintain equally, that in the day in which you admit those who deny the Incarnation to an equality of privileges, you remove the social life and order in which you live from the Incarnation to the basis of mere nature: and this is precisely what was foretold of the antichristian period. We have already seen that the third and special mark of Antichrist is the denial of the Incarnation; and if the nations of the world have been constituted by faith, upon the basis of the Incarnation, the national act which admits those who deny it to a social and political unity, is in fact a removal of the order of social life from the supernatural to the natural order: and this is what we see accomplishing. Once more I say, I am not now arguing against this; but I see in all these facts the verification of prophecy. Greater is the danger of a people which has so lost faith in the Incarnation, that it is necessary to give up the Christian order instituted by the providence of God. But such is the state of the world, and to this end we are rapidly advancing. We are told that Etna has one hundred and sixty craters. Besides the two vast mouths which, joined together, form the immense crater commonly so called, on all its sides it is perforated and honeycombed by channels and by mouths, from which in centuries past the lava has, from time to time, burst forth. I can find no better illustration of the state of Christendom at this moment. The Church of God rests upon the basis of natural society, on the foundations of the old Roman Empire, on the civilisation of the heathen nations of the world, which for a time has been consecrated, consolidated, preserved, raised, sanctified, transformed, by the action of faith and grace. The Church of God rests still upon that basis; but beneath the Church is working continually the mystery of iniquity which already wrought in the Apostles' time, and is culminating at this moment to its strength, and gaining the ascendency. What, I ask, was the French Revolution of 1789, with all its bloodshed, blasphemy, impiety, and cruelty, in all its masquerade of horror and of mockery,—what was it but an outbreak of the antichristian spirit —the lava from beneath the mountain? And what was the outbreak in 1830 and 1848 but precisely the same principle of Antichrist working beneath Christian society, forcing its way upwards? In the year 1848 it opened simultaneously its many mouths in Berlin, in Vienna, in Turin, in Florence, in Naples, and in Rome itself. In London, it heaved and struggled; but its time was not yet. What is all this but the spirit of lawlessness lifting itself against God and man,—the principle of schism, heresy, and infidelity running fused into one mass, and pouring itself forth wherever it can force its way, making craters for its stream wherever the Christian society becomes weak? And this, as it has gone on for centuries, so it will go on until the time shall come when "that which holds shall be taken out of the way."

We have already seen what it is that stands in the way of the ascendency of this principle of disorder. Now, visibly, this hindrance or barrier is weakening every day. It is weakening intellectually. The intellectual convictions of men are growing feebler; the Christian and Catholic civilisation is giving way before the natural material civilisation, which finds its supreme perfection in mere material prosperity; admitting within its sphere persons of every caste, or colour of belief, upon the principle that politics have nothing to do with the world to come,—that the government of nations is simply for their temporal wellbeing, for the protection of persons and of property, for the development of industry, and for the advancement of science; that is to say, for the cultivation of the natural order alone. This is the theory of civilisation which is becoming predominant every day. Catholic piety also is becoming weaker and weaker, and to such an extent, that there are nations still called Catholic in which the proportion to the mass of those who frequent the Holy Sacraments is hardly calculable: according as our Divine Lord has said, "Because iniquity hath abounded, the charity of many shall grow cold." * Again, the Christian society is everywhere becoming weaker—that is, the true Christian spirit and principle of society. The late M. de Tocqueville, who, as far as I can perceive, had no intention whatever to verify or establish what I am saying, writing upon democracy in America, points out the fact, that the tendency of every government in the world, and of every nation in the world, is to democracy; that is to say, to the diminution and exhaustion of the powers of government, and to the development of the licence of the popular will, so as to resolve all law into the will of the multitude. He points out that in France, in every successive half-century, a double revolution has carried society further towards democracy; that the same phenomena are to be seen in the whole Christian world. "Everywhere," he says, "we have seen the events of the life of nations turn to the advancement of democracy; all men have helped it onward by their efforts: they who designedly assisted its successes, and they who never thought of serving it; they who have fought for it, and they who are its declared enemies: all have been carried pell-mell in the same path, and all have laboured together; the one sort in spite of themselves,

* St. Matt. xxiv. 12.

the others without knowing it, as blind instruments in the hand of God. . . . This whole book has been written under the impression of a kind of religious fear produced in the mind of the author by the sight of this irresistible revolution, which for so many centuries marched onward over all obstacles, and which we see still at this day going forward through all the ruins it has made."* It is curious to place side by side with this the words of St. Hippolytus, written in the third century, who says that in the end of the world the Roman Empire shall pass εἰς δημοκρατίας, "into democracies."†

Again, another writer, a Spaniard of great intelligence and also of great faith, who lately died ambassador to Paris, Donoso Cortez, describing the state of society, said that Christian society is doomed, that it has to run its course, and become extinct; for the principles which are now in the ascendent are essentially antichristian. He drew out what is most manifest in the history of nations at this moment, namely, that there is a weakening of the principle of the ecclesiastical order everywhere, and that wheresoever the power of the Church over a nation is weakened, the temporal power is developed in a greater degree; so that nothing is more certain than

---

* De la Démocratie en Amérique, par Alexis de Tocqueville, vol. i. Introduction, pp. 8, 9.
† De Antichristo, xxvii.

that temporal despotism prevails especially in those countries where the power of the Church is depressed, and that the only security for liberty among the races of mankind is to be found in the freedom of the Church, and in its free action upon the government of the civil power. He says, " In giving up the empire of faith as dead, and in proclaiming the independence of the reason and of the will of man, society has rendered absolute, universal, and necessary the evil which was only relative, exceptional, and contingent. This period of rapid retrogression commenced in Europe with the restoration of paganism—philosophical, religious, and political. At this day the world is on the eve of the last of its restorations—the restoration of socialist paganism." *

Again the same writer says : " European society is dying. The extremities are cold: the heart will be soon. And do you know why it is dying? It is dying because it has been poisoned ; because God made it to be nourished with the substance of Catholic truth, and the empirical doctors have given it for food the substance of rationalism. It is dying because, like as man does not live by bread only, but by every word which comes out of the mouth of God, so societies do not perish by the sword only, but by every word which comes out of the mouth of their

---

* Lettre à M. de Montalembert, 4 juin 1849,—Œuvres, vol. i. p. 354.

philosophers. It is dying because error is killing it, and because society is now founded upon errors. Know, then, that all you hold as incontrovertible is false.

"The vital force of truth is so great, that if you were possessed of one truth,—one alone,—that truth might save you. But your fall is so profound, your decline is so radical, your blindness so complete, your nakedness so absolute, that even this one truth you have not. For this reason the catastrophe which must come will be in history the catastrophe above all. Individuals may still save themselves, because individuals may always be saved; but society is lost, not because it is yet in a radical impossibility of being saved, but because it has no will to save itself. There is no salvation for society, because we will not make our sons to be Christians, and because we are not true Christians ourselves. There is no salvation for society, because the Catholic spirit, the only spirit of life, does not quicken the whole; it does not quicken education, government, institutions, laws, and morals. To change the course of things in the state in which they are, I see too well would be the enterprise of giants. There is no power upon earth which, by itself, could reach this end, and hardly all the powers acting together could attain its accomplishment. I leave you to judge whether such co-operation is possible, and to what point, and to decide if, even admitting this possibility, the salvation of society would not be every way a true miracle." *

The last point, then, upon which I have to speak is this, that the barrier, or hindrance, to lawlessness will exist until it is taken out of the way. Now what is the meaning of the words, until it "be taken out of the way"? Who is to take it out of the way? Shall it be taken out of the way by the will of man? Shall it be taken out of the way by the mere casualty of events? Surely this is not the meaning. If the barrier which has hindered the development of the principle of antichristian disorder has been the Divine power of Jesus Christ our Lord, incorporated in the Church and guided by his Vicar, then no hand is mighty enough, and no will is sovereign enough, to take it out of the way, but only the hand and the will of the incarnate Son of God Himself. And therefore the interpretation of the Holy Fathers, with which I began, is fully and literally exact. It is the Divine power first in Providence, and then in His Church, and then both fused together, and continuing until the time shall come, the time foreseen and foreordained, for removing the barrier, in order to let in a new dispensation of His wisdom upon the earth, upon which I shall have to speak hereafter.

Now we have an analogy to this. The history of the Church, and the history of our Lord on earth,

* Polémique avec divers Journaux de Madrid, vol. i. 574-576.

run as it were in parallel. For three-and-thirty years the Son of God incarnate was in the world, and no man could lay hand upon him. No man could take Him, because His "hour was not yet come." There was an hour foreordained when the Son of God would be delivered into the hands of sinners. He foreknew it; He foretold it. He held it in His own hand, for He surrounded His person with a circle of His own Divine power. No man could break through that circle of omnipotence until the hour came, when by His own will He opened the way for the powers of evil. For this reason He said in the garden, "This is your hour, and the power of darkness."* For this reason, before He gave Himself into the hands of sinners, He exerted once more the majesty of His power, and when they came to take Him, He rose and said, "I am He,"† and "they went backward, and fell to the ground." Having vindicated His Divine Majesty, He delivered Himself into the hands of sinners. So too, He said, when He stood before Pilate, "Thou shouldst not have any power against Me, unless it were given thee from above."‡ It was the will of God; it was by the concession of the Father that Pilate had power over His incarnate Son. Again, He said, "Thinkest thou that I cannot ask My Father, and He will give me presently more than twelve

---

* St. Luke xxii. 53.   † St. John xviii. 5.
‡ St. John xix. 11.

legions of angels? how then shall the scripture be fulfilled?"* In like manner with His Church. Until the hour is come when the barrier shall, by the Divine will, be taken out of the way, no one has power to lay a hand upon it. The gates of hell may war against it; they may strive and wrestle, as they struggle now, with the Vicar of our Lord; but no one has the power to move Him one step, until the hour shall come when the Son of God shall permit, for a time, the powers of evil to prevail. That He will permit it for a time stands in the book of prophecy. When the hindrance is taken away, the man of sin will be revealed. Then will come the persecution of three years and a half, short, but terrible, during which the Church of God will return into its state of suffering, as in the beginning. But the imperishable Church of God, by its inextinguishable life derived from the pierced side of Jesus, which for three hundred years lived on through martyrdom, will live on still through the fires of the times of Antichrist.

These things are fulfilling fast, and it is good for us to keep them before our eyes: for the forerunners are already abroad—the weakness of the Holy Father; the murder of his armies, the invasion of his States, the betrayal of those who are nearest to him, the tyranny of those who are his sons; the joy, the exultation, the jubilee of Protestant countries and Pro-

* St. Matt. xxvi. 53, 54.

testant governments; the scorn, the contempt, the mockery, which is poured out upon his sacred and anointed head day by day in England. And there are Catholics who are scandalised at it; there are Catholics who talk against the temporal power of the Pope, either because they have been stunned by the clamours of a Protestant people, or because they are white-hearted, and have not courage to stand in the face of popular falsehood for an unpopular truth. The spirit of Protestant England—its lawlessness, its pride, its contempt, and its enmity to the Church of God— has made Catholics too to be cold-hearted, even when the Vicar of Jesus Christ is insulted. We have need, then, to be upon our guard. It shall happen once more with some, as it happened when the Son of God was in His Passion—they saw Him betrayed, bound, carried away, buffeted, blindfolded, and scourged; they saw Him carrying His Cross to Calvary, then nailed upon it, and lifted up to the scorn of the world; and they said, "If He be the king of Israel, let Him now come down from the cross, and we will believe Him."* So in like manner they say now, "See this Catholic Church, this Church of God, feeble and weak, rejected even by the very nations called Catholic. There is Catholic France, and Catholic Germany, and Catholic Italy, giving up this exploded figment of the temporal power of the Vicar of Jesus Christ." And

* St. Matt. xxvii. 42.

so, because the Church seems weak, and the Vicar of the Son of God is renewing the Passion of his Master upon earth, therefore we are scandalised, therefore we turn our faces from him. Where, then, is our faith? But the Son of God foretold these things when He said, "And now I have told you, before it come to pass; that when it shall come to pass, you may believe." *

* St. John xiv. 29.

LECTURE IV.

Before we enter upon the last subject which remains, let us take up the point at which we broke off in the last Lecture. It was this, that there are upon earth two great antagonists—on the one side, the spirit and the principle of evil; and on the other, the incarnate God manifested in His Church, but eminently in His Vicar, who is His representative, the depository of His prerogatives, and therefore His special personal witness, speaking and ruling in His Name. The office of the Vicar of Jesus Christ contains, in fulness, the Divine prerogatives of the Church: forasmuch as, being the special representative of the Divine Head, he bears all his communicable powers in the government of the Church on earth, solely and alone. The other bishops and pastors, who are united with him, and act in subordination to him, cannot act without him; but he may act alone, possessing a plenitude of power in himself. And further, the endowments of the body are the prerogatives of the head; and therefore the endowments which descend from the Divine Head of the Church upon the whole mystical body are centred in the head of that body upon earth; forasmuch as he stands in the place of the Incarnate Word as the minister and witness of the Kingdom of God among men. Now, it is against that person eminently and emphatically, as I said before, that the spirit of evil and of falsehood directs its assault; for if the head of the body be smitten, the body itself must die. "Smite the shepherd, and the sheep shall be scattered," was the old guile of the evil one, who smote the Son of God that he might scatter the flock. But that craft has been once tried, and foiled for ever; for in the death which smote the Shepherd, the flock was redeemed: and though the shepherd who is constituted in the place of the Son be smitten, the flock can be scattered no more. Three hundred years the world strove to cut off the line of the Sovereign Pontiffs; but the flock was never scattered: and so it shall be to the end. It is, nevertheless, against the Church of God, and above all against its Head, that all the spirits of evil in all ages, and, above all, in the present, direct the shafts of their enmity. We see, therefore, what it is that hinders the manifestation the supremacy, and the dominion of the spirit of evil and of disorder upon earth—namely, the constituted order of Christendom, the supernatural society of which the Catholic Church has been the creator, the bond of union, and the principle of conservation; and the head of that Church, who is eminently the principle of order—the centre of the Christian society which binds the nations of the world in peace. Now the subject which remains to us is far more difficult. It reaches into the future, and deals with agencies so transcendent and mysterious, that all I shall venture to do will be to sketch in outline what the broad and luminous prophecies of the sacred books set forth; without attempting to enter into minute details, which can only be interpreted by the event.

And further, as I said in the beginning, I shall not attempt anything, except under the direct guidance of the theologians of the Church, and of writers whose works have its approbation. As I have ventured hitherto nothing of my own, so until the end I shall pursue the same course.

What I have, then, to speak of is, the persecution of Antichrist, and finally his destruction.

First of all, let us begin with the twenty-fourth chapter of the holy Gospel according to St. Matthew, in which we read that our Divine Lord when He beheld the building of the Temple, said, " There shall not be left here a stone upon a stone that shall not be destroyed." And His disciples, when He was in the Mount of Olives, came to Him privately and said, " Tell us what will be the sign of Thy coming, and of the consummation of the world." They understood that the destruction of the Temple in Jerusalem and the end of the world should be part of one and the same action, and should take place at one and the same time. Now, as in nature we see mountains foreshortened one against another, so that the whole chain seems but one outline, so in the events of prophecy. There are here two different events which appear but one—the destruction of Jerusalem, and the end of the world. Our Divine Lord went on to tell them that there should come such a tribulation as had never yet been; and that unless those days were shortened, there should no flesh be saved; that for the sake of the elect those days should be shortened; that kingdom should rise against kingdom, and nation against nation, and there should be wars and pestilences and famines in divers places; that brethren should betray their brethren to death,* that His disciples should be persecuted for His name's sake, that all men should hate them, that they should be put to death, and that false Christs and false prophets should arise and should seduce many; that is, there should come false teachers, pretended Messias; and that in the midst of all these persecutions He himself would come to judgment—that, like as the lightning cometh out of the east, and appeareth even unto the west, so shall also the coming of the Son of Man be.

In this answer our Divine Lord spoke of two events—one, the destruction of Jerusalem, and the other, the end of the world. The one has been ful-

* St. Mark xiii.

filled, and the other is yet to come. Now three chief agents at this moment exist upon earth. First, there is the Catholic Church; next, there is the ancient people of God, the Jewish race, still preserved, as we have already seen, by a mysterious providence, for some future dispensation; and thirdly, there is the natural society of man without God, which took the form of paganism of old, and is taking the form of infidelity in the last days. These three are the ultimate agents in the history of the modern world: first, the natural society of mankind; next, the dispersion of the Jewish people; and, thirdly, the universal Church. The two last are the only bodies which interpenetrate into all nations, and have an unity distinct and independent of them. They have a greater power than any nation, and are direct and changeless antagonists. Now the Church has had to undergo already two persecutions, one from the hand of the Jews, and one also from the hand of the pagans. The writers of the early ages, the Fathers both of the East and of the West, foretold that, in the last age of the world, the Church will have to undergo a third persecution from the hands of an infidel world revolted from the Incarnate Word. And therefore the prophecy of St. Matthew reveals two events, or two actions. There is the event which is past, the type and the shadow of the event to come, and there is the event which is still future, at the end of the world; and all the persecutions that have ever been hitherto are no more than the forerunners and the types of the last persecution which shall be.

With these preliminary observations, let us begin the last part of our subject. What I have to speak of is the persecution which Antichrist shall inflict upon the Church of God. We have already seen reason to believe that as our Divine Lord delivered Himself into the hands of sinners when His time was come, and no man could lay hand upon Him, until of His own free will He delivered Himself over to their power, so in like manner it shall be with that Church of which He said, "Upon this rock will I build my Church, and the gates of hell shall not prevail against it." As the wicked did not prevail against Him even when they bound Him with cords, dragged Him to the judgment, blindfolded His eyes, mocked Him as a false King, smote Him on the head as a false Prophet, led Him away, crucified Him, and in the mastery of their power seemed to have absolute dominion over Him, so that He lay ground down and almost annihilated under their feet; and as, at that very time when He was dead and buried out of their sight, He was conqueror over all, and rose again the third day, and ascended into heaven, and was crowned, glorified, and invested with His royalty, and reigns supreme, King of kings and Lord of lords,—even so shall it be with His Church: though for a time persecuted, and to the eyes of man, overthrown and trampled on, dethroned, despoiled, mocked, and crushed, yet in that high time of triumph the gates of hell shall not prevail. There is in store for the Church of God a resurrection and an ascension, a royalty and a dominion, a recompense of glory for all it has endured. Like Jesus, it needs must suffer on the way to its crown; yet crowned it shall be with Him eternally. Let no one, then, be scandalised if the prophecy speak of sufferings to come. We are fond of imagining triumphs and glories for the Church on earth,—that the Gospel is to be preached to all nations, and the world to be converted, and all enemies subdued, and I know not what,—until some ears are impatient of hearing that there is in store for the Church a time of terrible trial: and so we do as the Jews of old, who looked for a conqueror, a king, and for prosperity; and when their Messias came in humility and in passion, they did not know Him. So, I am afraid, many among us intoxicate their minds with the visions of success and victory, and cannot endure the thought that there is a time of persecution yet to come for the Church of God. I will therefore point out as briefly as I can what appears in the events now around as to be leading on to this result.

1. The first sign or mark of this coming persecution is an indifference to truth. Just as there is a dead calm before a whirlwind, and as the waters over

a great fall run like glass, so before an outbreak there is a time of tranquillity. The first sign is indifference. The sign that portends more surely than any other the outbreak of a future persecution is a sort of scornful indifference to truth or falsehood. Ancient Rome in its might and power adopted every false religion from all its conquered nations, and gave to each of them a temple within its walls. It was sovereignly and contemptuously indifferent to all the superstitions of the earth. It encouraged them; for each nation had its own proper superstition, and that proper superstition was a mode of tranquillising, of governing, and of maintaining in subjection the people who were indulged by building a temple within its gates. In like manner we see the nations of the Christian world at this moment gradually adopting every form of religious contradiction—that is, giving it full scope, and, as it is called, perfect toleration; not recognising any distinctions of truth or falsehood between one religion or another, but leaving all forms of religion to work their own way. Miserable is the state of the world in which ten thousand poisons grow round one truth; miserable is the state of any country where truth is only tolerated. This is a state of great spiritual and intellectual danger.

Let us see the result. First of all, the divine voice of the Church of God is thereby entirely ignored. They see no distinction between a doctrine of faith and a human opinion. Both are allowed to have free way. There are mixed together doctrines of faith with every form of heresy, until, as in England, we have all conceivable forms of belief, from the Council of Trent in all its rigour and in all its perfection on the one hand, to the *Catechism of Positive Religion* on the other. We have every form of opinion started, and freely allowed, from the two extremes; the one of which is the worship of God in Unity and Trinity, the Son incarnate for us; and the other, the denial of God, and the worship of humanity. Next, denying and ignoring of course the divine voice of the Church, the civil governor must ignore the divine unity of the Church, and admit every form of separation, or system, or division all mingled together; so that the people are crumbled into religious sects and religious divisions, and the law of unity is altogether lost. Then, again, all positive truth, as such, is rejected; and it is rejected, because who shall say who is right and who is wrong, if there be no Divine teacher? If there be no Divine judge, who shall say what is true and what is false between conflicting religious opinions? A state that has separated itself from the unity of the Church, and has thereby lost the guidance of the Divine teacher, is unable to determine by any of its tribunals, civil or ecclesiastical, as it may continue to call them, what is true and what is false in a controverted question of religion; and then, as we know, there grows up an intense hatred of what is called dogmatism, that is, of any positive truth, anything definite, anything final, anything which has precise limits, any form of belief which is expressed in particular definitions—all this is utterly distasteful to men who on principle encourage all forms of religious opinion. In fact, we are coming to the state of Festus, who, when he heard that the Jews had an accusation against St. Paul, reported that he could find " no question which seemed ill " to him, because they were questions of superstition, and " about one Jesus deceased, whom Paul affirmed to be alive." * Now this is just the state of indifference to which the civil governors of the world are gradually reducing themselves, and the governments they administer, and the people they govern.

2. The next step which is also a fulfilment of the prophecies is the persecution of the truth. When Rome in ancient days legalised every idolatry throughout the whole of the Roman Empire, there was one religion which was called a *religio illicita*, an unlawful religion, and there was one society which was called a *societas illicita*, or an unlawful society. They might worship the twelve gods of Egypt, or Jupiter Capitolinus, or Dea Roma; but they might not worship the God of heaven, they might not worship God revealed in His Son. The

* Acts xx. 18, 19.

Romans did not believe in the Incarnation; and that one religion which was alone true was the only religion that was not tolerated. There were the priests of Jupiter, of Cybele, of Fortune, and of Vesta; there were all manner of sacred confraternities, and orders, and societies; but there was one society which was not permitted to exist, and that was the Church of the living God. In the midst of this universal toleration, there was one exception made with the most peremptory exactness, to exclude the truth and the Church of God from the world. Now this is what must again inevitably come to pass, because the Church of God is inflexible in the mission committed to it. The Catholic Church will never compromise a doctrine; it will never allow two opposite doctrines to be taught within its pale; it will never obey the civil governor when he pronounces judgment in things that are spiritual. The Catholic Church is bound by the Divine law to suffer martyrdom rather than compromise a doctrine, or obey the law of the civil governor which violates the conscience; and more than this, it is not only bound to offer a passive disobedience, which may be done in a corner, and therefore not detected, and because not detected not punished; but the Catholic Church cannot be silent; it cannot hold its peace; it cannot cease to preach the doctrines of Revelation, not only of the Trinity and of the Incarnation, but likewise of the Seven Sacraments, and of the infallibility of the Church of God, and of the necessity of unity, and of obedience to the Holy See as to a sovereign principle of truth: and because it will not be silent, and cannot compromise, and will not obey in matters that are of its own Divine prerogative, therefore it stands alone in the world; for there is not another Church so called, nor any community professing to be a Church, which does not submit, or obey, or hold its peace, when the civil governors of the world command. It is not ten years since we heard of a decision on the matter of baptism, involving the doctrine of original sin on the one hand, and the doctrine of preventing grace on the other; and because a civil judge pronounced that it was lawful in the Established Church of England for men without punishment to teach two contradictory doctrines, bishops, priests, and people were content that it should be so: or, at least, they said, "We cannot do otherwise; the civil power will allow men to preach both: what can we do? We are persecuted, and therefore we hold our peace; we go on ministering under a civil law which compels us to endure that the man who preaches before us in the morning, or the man who shall preach after us in the afternoon, may preach a doctrine in diametrical contradiction to that which we know to be the revealed truth of God; and because the civil governors have determined it so, we are not responsible, and the Anglican Church is not responsible, because it is persecuted." Now this is the characteristic difference between a human system established by the civil law and the Church of God. Would it be permitted in the Church which is Catholic and Roman, that I should now deny that any child baptized receives the infusion of regenerating grace? What would become of me by to-morrow morning? You know perfectly well that if I were to depart one jot or one tittle from the Holy Catholic faith, delivered by the Divine voice of the Church of God, I should be immediately suspended, and no civil governor, or power in the world, could restore me to the exercise of my faculties; no civil judge or potentate on earth could re-instate me in the administration of the Sacraments, until the spiritual authority of the Church permitted me to do so.

This, then, is the characteristic difference, which must one day bring down upon the Church, in all countries where this spirit of indifference has established itself, a persecution of the civil power. And for a further reason, because the difference between the Catholic Church and every other society is this: other societies are of voluntary formation; that is, people unite themselves to a particular body, and, if they do not like it on better knowledge, they go their way: they become Baptists, or Anabaptists, or Episcopalians, or Unitarians, or Presbyterians, until they find something which they do not like in these systems; and then they go their way, and either unite themselves to some other body or remain unattached; because these societies have no claim to govern the will,—all that they profess to do is to teach. They are like the ancient schools, and their teaching is a kind of Christian philosophy. They put their doctrines before those who are willing to listen, and if they listen, and, by good fortune, agree with them, they remain with them: if not, they go their way. But where is the government over the will? Can they say, "In the name of God, and under pain of mortal sin, you must believe that God was incarnate, and that our incarnate Lord offers Himself in sacrifice upon the altar, that the Sacraments instituted by the Son of God are seven, and that they all convey the grace of the Holy Ghost"? Unless they have an authority over the will as well as over the intelligence they are only a school, and not a kingdom. Now this is a character entirely wanting in every society that cannot claim to govern in the name of our Divine Lord, and to teach with a Divine voice; and therefore the Church of God differs from every other society in this particular, that it is not only a communion of people who voluntarily unite together, but that it is a kingdom. It has a legislature; the line of its councils for eighteen hundred years have sat, deliberated, and decreed with all the solemnity and more than the majesty of an imperial parliament. It has an executive which carries out and enforces the decrees of those councils with all the calmness and more than the peremptory decision of an imperial will. The Church of God, therefore, is an empire within an empire; and the governors and princes of this world are jealous of it for that very reason. They say, "*Nolumus hunc regnare super nos*"—"we will not have this man to reign over us." It is precisely because the Son of God, when He came, established a kingdom upon earth, that therefore, in every land, in every nation, the Catholic Church governs with the authority of the universal Church of God. Therefore it is that ten years back the atmosphere was rent and tormented by the uproar of "Papal aggression." The natural instinct of the civil rulers knew that it was not a mere Christian philosophy wafted from foreign lands, but a spiritual power and a spiritual sovereignty. For this reason also, the extreme liberal school—those who claim toleration for every form of opinion, and who teach that the office of the civil governor is never to enter into controversies of religion, but that all men should be left free in their belief, and the conscience of all men be at liberty before God—even they make one exception, and, in the strangest contradiction to all their principles, or, at least, their professions, maintain that as the Catholic Church is not only a form of doctrine, but also a power or government, it must be excepted from the general toleration. And this is precisely the point of future collision. It is the very reason why the Archbishops of Cologne, Turin, Cagliari, and the like, went the other day into exile; why nineteen Sees are, at this moment, vacant in Sardinia. Why, in Italy, Bishops are, at this day, cast out from their Episcopal thrones; it is for this reason that in this land the Protestant religion is established instead of Catholic truth, and that thrones once filled by the Bishops of the universal Church are now occupied by those whom the royalties of England, and not the authority of the Vicar of Jesus Christ, have chosen and set up. It is the same old contest, old as Christianity itself, which has been from the beginning, first with pagan, and then with heretic, and then with schismatic, and then with infidel, and will continue to the end. The day is not far off, when the nations of the world, now so calm and peaceful in the stillness of their universal indifference, may easily be roused, and penal laws once more may be found in their statute-books.

3. This leads on plainly to the marks which the prophet gives of the persecution of the last days. Now there are three things which he has recorded. The first, that the continual sacrifice shall be taken away; the next, that the sanctuary shall be occupied by the abomination which maketh desolate; the third, that, "the strength" and "the stars," as he described

it, shall be cast down. And these are the only three I will notice.

Now, first of all, what is this "taking away of the continual sacrifice"?

It was taken away in type at the destruction of Jerusalem. The sacrifice of the Temple, that is, of the lamb, morning and evening, in the Temple of God, was entirely abolished with the destruction of the Temple itself. But the Prophet Malachias says:* "From the rising of the sun even to the going down, my name is great among the Gentiles; and in every place there is sacrifice, and there is offered to my name a clean oblation." This passage of the prophet has been interpreted by the Fathers of the Church, beginning with St. Irenæus, St. Justin Martyr, and I know not how many besides, to be the sacrifice of the Holy Eucharist, the true Paschal Lamb, which came in the place of the type—namely, the sacrifice of Jesus Himself on Calvary, renewed perpetually and continued for ever in the sacrifice on the altar. Now has that continual sacrifice been taken away? That which was typical of it in old days has been already taken away. But has the reality been taken away? The Holy Fathers who have written upon the subject of Antichrist, and have interpreted these prophecies of Daniel, say that towards the end of the world, during the reign of Antichrist, the public offer-

* Mal. i. 11.

ing of the Holy Sacrifice for a time will cease.* Has there as yet ever come to pass anything which may be called an instalment or a forerunner of such an event as this? Look into the East. The Mahometan superstition, which arose in Arabia, and swept over Palestine and Asia Minor, the region of the Seven Churches, and Egypt, the north of Africa—the home of St. Augustine, St. Cyprian, St. Optatus—and finally penetrated into Constantinople, where soon it became dominant, has in every place prohibited and suppressed the worship and sacrifice of Jesus Christ. The Mahometan superstition at this moment holds for its mosques a multitude of Christian churches, in which the continual sacrifice is already taken away, and the altar utterly destroyed. In Alexandria and in Constantinople there stand churches built for Christian worship, into which the foot of no Christian has ever entered since the continual sacrifice was swept away. Surely in this we see, in part at least, the fulfilment of this prophecy; so much so, that many interpreters will have it that Mahomet is the Antichrist, and that none other is to come. No doubt he was one of the many forerunners and types of the Antichrist that shall be. Now let us look into the Western world: has the continual sacrifice been taken away in any other land?—for instance, in all those churches of Protestant Germany which were once

* Malvenda, lib. viii. c. 4, &c.

Catholic, where the holy sacrifice of the Mass was daily offered ?—throughout Norway, and Sweden, and Denmark, and one half of Switzerland, where there are a multitude of ancient Catholic churches—throughout England, in the cathedrals and the parish churches of this land, which were built simply as shrines of Jesus present in the Holy Eucharist, as sanctuaries raised for the offering of the Holy Sacrifice ? What is the characteristic mark of the Reformation, but the rejection of the Mass, and all that belongs to it, as declared in the Thirty-nine Articles of the Church of England to be blasphemous fables and dangerous deceits ? The suppression of the continual sacrifice is, above all, the mark and characteristic of the Protestant Reformation. I need not stay to speak of the new and vigorous life that has sprung up in these very countries simultaneously with the fulfilment of this prophecy, nor of how the Holy Sacrifice, taken away from the old sanctuaries, appears anew on altars that are erected and multiplied every day, to the joy of the faithful and the confusion of the unbeliever. Nevertheless, this prophecy of Daniel has already its fulfilment both in the East and West,—in the two wings, as it were; while in the heart of Christendom the Holy Sacrifice is offered still. What is the great flood of infidelity, revolution, and anarchy, which is now sapping the foundations of Christian society, not only in France, but in Italy, and encompassing Rome, the centre and sanctuary of the Catholic Church, but the abomination which desolates the sanctuary, and takes away the continual sacrifice? The secret societies have long ago undermined and honeycombed the Christian society of Europe, and are at this moment struggling onward towards Rome, the centre of all Christian order in the world.

The Protestant spirit of England, and the schismatical spirit even of countries Catholic in name, is at this moment urging on the great anticatholic movement of Italy. Hostility to the Holy See is the true and governing motive. And thus we come to the third mark, the casting down of " the Prince of Strength ;" that is, the Divine authority of the Church, and especially of him in whose person it is embodied, the Vicar of Jesus Christ. God has invested him with sovereignty, and given to him a home and a patrimony on earth. The world is in arms to depose him, and to leave him no place to lay his head. Rome and the Roman States are the inheritance of the Incarnation. The world is resolved to drive the Incarnation off the earth. It will not suffer it to possess so much as to set the sole of its foot upon. This is the true interpretation of the anticatholic movement of Italy and England: " *Tolle hunc de terra.*" The dethronement of the Vicar of Christ is the dethronement of the hierarchy of the universal Church, and the public rejection of the Presence and Reign of Jesus.

4. Now, if I am obliged to enter somewhat into the future, I shall confine myself to tracing out a very general outline. The direct tendency of all the events we see at this moment is clearly this, to overthrow Catholic worship throughout the world. Already we see that every Government in Europe is excluding religion from its public acts. The civil powers are desecrating themselves: government is without religion; and if government be without religion, education must be without religion. We see it already in America and in France. It has been again and again attempted in England. The result of this can be nothing but the reëstablishment of mere natural society; that is to say, the governments and the powers of the world, which for a time were subdued by the Church of God to a belief in Christianity, to obedience to the laws of God, and to the unity of the Church, having revolted from it and desecrated themselves, have relapsed into their natural state.

The prophet Daniel, in the twelfth chapter, says that in the time of the end many shall be chosen and made white, and shall be tried as fire; and the wicked shall deal wickedly, and none of the wicked shall understand, but the learned shall understand; that is, many who have known the faith shall abandon it, by apostasy. "Some of the learned shall fall;"* that is, they shall fall from their fidelity to God. And how shall this come to pass? Partly by fear, partly by deception, partly by cowardice; partly because they cannot stand for unpopular truth in the face of popular falsehood; partly because the overruling contemptuous public opinion, as in such a country as this, and in France, so subdues and frightens Catholics, that they dare not avow their principles, and at last, dare not hold them. They become admirers and worshippers of the material prosperity of Protestant countries. They see the commerce, the manufactures, the agriculture, the capital, the practical science, the irresistible armies, the fleets that cover the sea, and they come flocking to adore, and say, "Nothing is so great as this great country of Protestant England." And so they give up their faith, and become materialists, seeking for the wealth and power of this world, dazzled and overpowered by the greatness of a country which has cast off its fidelity to the Church.

5. Now the last result of all this will be a persecution, which I will not attempt to describe. It is enough to remind you of the words of our Divine Master: "Brother shall betray brother to death;" it shall be a persecution in which no man shall spare his neighbour. But there is One Power which will destroy all antagonists; there is One Person who will

* Dan. xi. 35.

break down and smite small as the dust of the summer threshing-floor all the enemies of the Church, for it is He who will consume His enemies "with the Spirit of His mouth," and destroy them "with the brightness of His coming." It seems as if the Son of God were jealous lest any one should vindicate His authority. He has claimed the battle to Himself; He has taken up the gage which has been cast down against Him; and prophecy is plain and explicit that the last overthrow of evil will be His; that it will be wrought by no man, but by the Son of God; that all the nations of the world may know that He, and He alone, is King, and that He, and He alone, is God.

Thus far I have wished to show, first, that the vaunt and the boast and the triumph of the enemies of the Holy See at the present weakness and isolation of the Temporal State of Rome is without foundation or sense. Let the present revolution prosper ten times more than it ever has or will, we are prepared for any result. Let the enemies of the Church usurp Rome ten times, as they have already in ages past, the Holy See and the Vicar of Jesus Christ are beyond their power. Next, I desire to give courage and strength to some to whom adversity is a temptation and failure a stone of offence. And lastly, to meet in full front the senseless interpretations of prophecy by Protestants, who, confounding all things, make Christ and Antichrist to change places.* From which, too, it is evident that the hostility of Protestantism and of the Revolution against the Church in Rome is a prelude of Antichrist, and a sign of antagonism to the kingdom of Jesus Christ on earth. Nevertheless the filial love and devoted loyalty of the Roman people to their Father, Pastor, and Prince has never been more heartfelt, though the violence and terror of evil may restrain its accents. But no words of mine can express this as it ought; and I therefore recite the words of one who, above all, knows the heart of his people and of Rome.

"Here we know not," says the Sovereign Pontiff, "how to pass in silence the constant evidence of

---

* In reducing the ten Lectures which compose this volume to the form originally intended, viz. that of a popular exposition of the Temporal Power of the Holy See, I have excluded digressions which were disproportioned to the main subject and foreign to my purpose. They were applicable only to the time and place where the discourses were given, and rendered fitting only by the incessant controversies and absurd misinterpretations of Holy Scripture used as weapons of controversy. If there should be need, I will treat this subject in a separate form. In the meantime students may find these authorities sufficient:

Malvenda, de Antichristo, lib. iv. c. 5. Romæ, 1604.
Lessius, de Antichristo, dem. xii.
Bellarm. de Summo Pontifice, lib. iv. c. 4.
Viegas, de Apoc. c. xviii.
Cornel. à Lapide, in Apoc. c. xviii.
Herinx, Summa Theol. pars iv. quæst. 2, de Antichristo.
See especially Suarez, Defensio Fidei Catholicæ, lib. v. c. vii. 9, c. xv. 17, c. xxi. 7.

real affection, of unalterable fidelity, which the Roman people have lavished towards us. Desirous of giving striking proof of the tenacity with which it firmly holds itself attached to us, to this Apostolic See, and to this temporal sovereignty which belongs to us, it repels and condemns with the greatest energy the culpable intrigues and endeavours of those who seek to lay snares in its path and to spread trouble in its bosom. Have not you yourselves, Venerable Brethren, witnessed over and over again the sincere, undisguised, and cordial manifestations by which this Roman people, which we so much love, has displayed its sentiment of traditional faith—a faith which deservedly merits the greatest praise?"*

Now I have not attempted to point out what shall be the future events except in outline, and I have never ventured to designate who shall be the person that shall accomplish them. Of this I know nothing; but I am enabled with the most perfect certainty, from the Word of God, and from the interpretations of the Church, to point out the great principles which are in conflict on either side. I began by showing you that the Antichrist, and the antichristian movement, has these marks: first, schism from the Church of God; secondly, denial of its Divine and infallible voice; and thirdly, denial of the Incarnation. It is, therefore, the direct and mortal enemy of the One

* Allocution of the Sovereign Pontiff Pius IX., Sept. 30, 1861.

Holy Catholic and Roman Church—the unity from which all schism is made; the sole organ of the Divine voice of the Spirit of God; the shrine and sanctuary of the Incarnation and of the continual sacrifice.

I have spoken of the great subject so vital and dear to all Catholics at this moment, the Temporal Power of the Holy See. I have endeavoured to show its divine institution and intention, its divine aim and mission and ministration in creating the order of Christian Europe, and the consequence of the present conflict of the civil powers against it.

This naturally led me to consider the nature of that conflict, and to trace it to its origin. The prophecies of St. Paul, as we have seen, describe its principle and operation; and the history of Christianity shows that it has a continuous activity, which, under its many forms, has always assailed the Church of God. The conflict of this age against the Holy See is only another change of form: the principle is identical. Now this has led me to the verge of a question on which, as all the Theologians of the Church who treat of this matter have spoken, it is hardly possible to be silent. I mean the last persecution of the Church, which is still to come. With this I am compelled to break off; and this abrupt ending may seem to imply that there is no glorious future, no reign of sovereign peace in store for the Church on earth. I hope, therefore, to add other

Lectures in order to bring out the imperishable life, the indivisible unity, the perpetual visibleness, the indissoluble sovereignty of the Church. All its sufferings have passed over it as mists over the sun, in the orb and glory of which there is neither " transmutatio nec vicissitudinis obumbratio," *—neither "change nor shadow of vicissitude." All its future trials will in like manner pass over it as a transient cloud,—dark, but soon gone,—revealing the divine prerogatives and sovereignty of the Church in a more luminous splendour. In the history of its reign on earth these passing moments are as nothing. The waves go over the ship, and they are not; but the ship, with unchanged course, bears on. So with the Kingdom of Jesus upon earth : it is "regnum immobile ;" † ever expanding, pushing out its frontiers, and unfolding its prerogatives upon the world. Such as He founded it, such it shall be at His coming; but full with the glories and accumulated powers of its long warfare upon earth.

Let no one say, then, that these Lectures have a desponding tone. Sorrowful, I admit; but desponding, it could not be. Sorrowful, I am aware they are ; and who can be otherwise than sorrowful, when he sees the havoc of infidelity and anarchy in the fair provinces of Christian Europe,—when he reflects on the loss of souls, the growing evils of the world, and

---

* St. James i. 17.   † Heb. xii. 28.

the dishonours of the most Precious Blood? It is impossible, I think, to look upon the present crisis of the Holy See without remembering the agony in the Garden, and the Divine prevision of the Son of God, to which all these things were present, when He said, "My soul is sorrowful even unto death."* It seems to me, also, that the tone of the Supreme Pontiffs has always been a tone of supernatural sorrow over the waywardness of men, and the sins of the Christian world. I know nothing more pathetic than the writings of St. Gregory the Great, unless it be the majestic and moving encyclical letters of Pius IX. Such a sorrow every Catholic ought to breathe; and if he does not partake of it, he ought carefully to examine himself, to find the reason of his exemption from a sorrow which seems inseparable from a love of the holy Catholic and Roman Church. I acknowledge, also, another cause of sorrow was present in my mind even more powerfully than perhaps I was altogether aware. I do not know how any one can treat the trials of the Holy See as an abstraction. To me, at least, they come incorporated in the person, and visible in the image, of the most august and supernatural presence I have ever known in life. The sufferings of the Holy See are the sufferings of the Holy Father. It is not the "cathedra Petri," but the person of Pius IX., that comes before us when we turn our

* St. Matt. xxvi. 38.

eyes and hearts upon this most unnatural warfare of sons against their Father. The sovereign dignity and the paternal sweetness of countenance, manner, and voice; the playfulness, simplicity, and tenderness of the saintly countenance and tone of him who for ten years has deigned to receive, direct, encourage, and console me in the most trying season of my life, were before me, even more vividly than at other times, when I was contemplating the present and the possible future of the Holy See. A sorrowful tone, therefore, I readily acknowledge. If it is more so than befits the subject and the time, I acknowledge also the fault, and trust only that it may be venial. But of desponding I cannot feel guilty. To despond is contrary to faith. It is no manliness or courage to be hopeful because of visible success, and no despondency to be grave and forecasting in the presence of adversity. I see neither courage nor prudence in being afraid to measure our antagonists or to see their power. True courage—manly and Christian—seems to me to rest not upon numbers, or resources, or events, or prosperous issues, still less on a delusive hopefulness, but upon truths, and principles, and laws of the supernatural order, and the promises of God. When these are "for us, who is against us?"* What matters the rising of a thousand revolutions, or the temporary successes of ten thousand apostates?

* Rom. viii. 31.

The kingdom of God is divine, and its victory and glory are sure as the presence of Jesus upon earth.

I should indeed be sorry to write a line in a tone to discourage even one simple faithful soul; but I would do even this for a moment, if in so doing I could purify our confidence of the low, human, unreasoning, unilluminated, and almost boastful and defiant tone too commonly heard. This seems to me to be "ex sanguinibus, et ex voluntate carnis, et ex voluntate viri,"*—of man, and of flesh and blood, not of faith or of the Spirit of God. "Justus autem meus ex fide vivet." † We know by the light of Faith that all things are working out the greater glory of Jesus, and of His Church on earth. The confidence we have in the stability of nature, the revolutions of the firmament, the laws of gravitation, the return of seasons and of tides, is not more changeless than our consciousness that the one Holy Catholic and Roman Church is even now achieving, through passion and the cross, the victories of Jesus upon earth. And as the glories of Jesus were more and more revealed as He approached nearer to His Cross, and as the Cross itself was but the prelude of the Resurrection, and of the fuller manifestation of His kingdom and of His royalties, so is it with the Church, which in all things is conformed to His life of passion and of sovereignty. The prompting of our natural hearts, when we hear

* St. John i. 13.   † Heb. x. 56.

of the sufferings of those we love, is to speak with an impatient sorrow; as Peter, when Jesus took His disciples and told them that the Son of Man "must suffer many things, and be rejected by the ancients, by the high priests, and the Scribes, and be killed; and after three days rise again. And He spoke the word openly; and Peter, taking Him, began to rebuke Him."*

We too are ready to say, "This be far from Thee, Lord; this shall not be unto Thee." † Yet Jesus did not accept this manifestation of a too natural love. His words of rebuke have a divine energy, intended to teach us not to trust our human affections in judging of His supernatural dispensations. "Go behind Me, Satan, because thou savourest not the things that are of God, but that are of men." ‡

And now to make an end. Men have need to look to their principles. They have to make a choice between two things, between faith in a teacher speaking with an infallible voice, governing the unity which now, as in the beginning, knits together the nations of the world, or the spirit of fragmentary Christianity, which is the source of disorder, and ends in unbelief. Here is the simple choice to which we are all brought; and between them we must make up our minds.

The events of every day are carrying men further

---

* St. Mark viii. 31.   † St. Matt. xvi. 22.
‡ St Mark viii. 33.

and further in the career on which they have entered. Every day men are becoming more and more divided. These are times of sifting. Our Divine Lord is standing in the Church: "His fan is in His hand, and He will thoroughly cleanse His floor, and He will gather the grain into His barn, and will burn up the chaff with unquenchable fire." * It is a time of trial, when "some of the learned shall fall," and those only shall be saved who are steadfast to the end. The two great antagonists are gathering their forces for the last conflict;—it may not be in our day, it may not be in the time of those who come after us; but one thing is certain, that we are as much put on our trial now as they will be who live in the time when it shall come to pass. For as surely as the Son of God reigns on high, and will reign "until He has put all His enemies under His feet," so surely every one that lifts a heel or directs a weapon, a tongue, or a pen, against His faith, His Church, or His Vicar upon earth, will share the judgment which is laid up for the Antichrist whom he serves.

* St. Matt. iii. 12.

PART THIRD.

The last Glories of the Holy See greater than the first.

LECTURE I.

*"Great shall be the glory of this last house more than of the first."—*AGGEUS *ii. 10.*

THE Church is Jesus Himself; He is its Head, and it is His body; its fortunes are His fortunes, and its sufferings His sufferings; its teaching is His voice; its Sacraments are the touch of His hand; its visible Head is His Vicar; and all that befalls the Church on earth is shared by the Son of God. The Church of God, then, ought to be dear to us for His sake; for all that befalls it affects the Sacred Heart; and we cannot better make reparation to the Sacred Heart of our Divine Lord than by fidelity, even unto death, to the Church of God.

I have at other times spoken without reserve, and perhaps with somewhat too much of boldness, on the sufferings of the Church. I do not say on its dangers, for dangers there cannot be. Who ever heard of the dangers of Jesus? We have heard of the Passion of Jesus; and so we may speak of the suffering of His Church. But in danger the Church cannot be. The Church is the Church of God, and man is under His feet. Man can have no dominion over it. I have spoken, then, in this tone, first, because there is a mischievous and subtil error creeping into the hearts of many, that prosperity in this world is the test of God's favour,—which is Judaism, not Christianity. The Cross of our Lord has taught us that suffering is the sign of His presence. To look upon adversity in this world as a token of Divine displeasure, with Calvary before us, is a heresy. This language, then, is necessary to awaken in our hearts the perpetual consciousness that, if the Church of God to-morrow were to be crucified, and the world were to be supreme, it would yet be the mystical Body of Jesus; and if the world to-morrow were triumphant, and were to boast its sovereignty for a time, it would still be the kingdom of Antichrist.

But we have other things in store. And I would now speak to you on another theme, more bright and joyful indeed, but not more true, and hardly more necessary; and that is, upon the glories of the Holy See in the latter days—glories greater than the first. We read in Holy Writ that the elders and people of Israel wept when they saw the second temple, which was built after the captivity of Babylon, for they remembered the glories and the splendour of the first house built by their fathers. Therefore the prophet Aggeus said, "Great shall be the glory of this last house more than of the first." So of the Holy See in the latter days of its conflict on earth: greater shall be its glories even than in its earlier times,—greater even than in the days of its martyred Pontiffs, than in the days of its first supernatural powers and miracles, than in the days when first from the Holy See went forth a spiritual agency to convert the world and to subdue the empire to itself,—greater even than these shall be the glories of its latter days. For as the light of the daybreak is in the splendour of noontide, so the glories of its morning shall be found full and resplendent in its latter times. And as the power and flexibility of youth is to be found in the maturity of manhood, so the Pontiffs of the last ages shall be invested with the majesty and glory of the first.

The subject, then, on which I would speak is this the imperishable vitality, the invincible tenacity of endurance,—those two singular and Divine endowments of the Holy See, which have been always as time runs on, which are now, and shall ever be more and more, luminously manifested to the world. The vitality and endurance of the first three centuries of martyrdom was but the prelude of that which has sustained the Holy See in the last days of its conflict.

In order to bring this out more clearly, I would bid you first to remember that what is called the "temporal power" of the Pope contains in itself two distinct elements. The first is, the sovereignty inherent in his own person;* and the second is, the

---

* Suarez, in treating of the question, "Utrum Summus Pontifex omni jure divino et humano ab omni jurisdictione secularium prin-

local sovereignty over the State which he holds. These are two distinct things. His own personal sovereignty consists in this: first, that as the Vicar and representative of Jesus Christ, who is King of kings and Lord of lords, to whose hands all power in heaven and earth is given, he is liberated by

cipum exemptus sit," says: "Quamvis privilegium exemptionis commune sit Summo Pontifici cum reliquis clericis, cum ipse non solum clericus sit sed etiam clericorum et totius ecclesiæ Princeps et caput; tamen quia in illo propter singularem eminentiam notior est talis privilegii origo, et quia illius cognitio parare potest viam ad investigandam originem immunitatis aliorum ecclesiasticorum, ideo prius de Papa in particulari sermonem instituimus. De quo etiam hæretici non negant, nunc de facto exemptum esse ab omni sæculari potestate, quia ipse cum Pontificatu conjunctum habet temporale regnum, in quo superiorem non recognoscit, quia vero regnum istud non a Deo immediate, sed hominum devotione, vel alio simili humano titulo consecutus est, ideo talis exemptio non est per se conjuncta cum Pontificia dignitate nec ex divino jure, sed ex humano ducit originem vel certe supposito tali statu temporalis Principis ex natura rei sequitur, sicut in aliis Regibus qui exempti sunt ex vi sui status, quia non habent superiorem. Unde ad respondendum quæstioni propositæ, præscindenda est Regia dignitas a persona Pontificis et solum ut Pontifex considerandus est, sicut fuerunt Petrus et successores ejus ante Constantinum. Dicendum ergo est Summum Pontificem ex divino jure habere exemptionem et immunitatem ab omni judicio ac jurisdictione sæculari etiam Imperatorum et Regum. Hanc assertionem tenent in primis omnes Catholici Doctores, qui generaliter affirmant exemptionem hanc in toto Ecclesiastico statu esse de jure divino quos cap. 8 referemus. Præter eos vero, qui de inferioribus, vel id negant, vel dubii sunt, de Summo Pontifice propter ejus singularem dignitatem id ingenue fatetur Soto; idem sentiunt Bannes, Cajetanus, Turrecremata, Bellarminus, Molina, Valentia, Henricus, Driedo." Suarez, Defensio Fidei Catholicæ, &c., lib. iv. cap. 4, 1-3.

Divine right from all civil and temporal subjection to any ruler or prince on earth.* Thus he is in himself a personal sovereign, and can be subject to none; and thus, also, he has, in virtue of his Pontificate, a Divine authority over all other powers,† personal or princely, that can be found among men; forasmuch as when our Divine Lord said to Peter, "Feed My sheep," He gave the whole world into his hands; He committed to him, not only the direction of individuals one by one, but the direction of families, of households, of all the collective forms of natural society. The Church of God is the guide not only of the individual conscience in relation to itself, but in all its manifold orders and relations; not only of the child to the parent, but of the parent to the child. The Church of God guides, therefore, the family and the household; and if the family and the household, then nations and peoples. For what are the races and nations of the earth, but the families of mankind multiplied and expanded? What are kingdoms and empires, but the families of man aggregated together? And as the Church of God guides the father of a household, so it guides the ruler of a kingdom. Our Divine Lord committed to Peter and his successors the direction and guidance of the civil order which should arise in the world, of nations and their princes. It is his Divine office to see, and his duty to enforce,

* Suarez, *ubi supra*.   † *Ibid.*

obedience to the faith and to the laws of God. It is his official duty, therefore, to judge and to pronounce on the acts of individuals and peoples, of nations and their princes. The sole tribunal on earth which can guide and direct the consciences of men is the Church of God, and this office centres in its Head. This, then, is the personal sovereignty which is inherent in the Pontificate of the Vicar of Jesus Christ. The local sovereignty is over that state, territory, and people which the providence of God has committed to him. No one can read its history without perceiving that it was given by the same Divine will and the same Divine hand from which he received also his personal sovereignty in the beginning, and his liberation from all subjection. The conversion of the empire to Christianity, and then its removal, its banishment into the far East, freed the Vicar of Jesus Christ from temporal subjection; and then, by the action of the same Providence, he was clothed with the prerogatives of a true and proper local sovereignty over that state and territory and people so committed to his charge. From that hour, which I might say was fifteen hundred years ago, or, to speak within limit, I will say was twelve hundred, the Supreme Pontiff has been a true and proper sovereign, exercising the prerogatives of royalty committed to him by the will of God over the people to whom he is father in all things both spiritual and temporal.

This order, divinely founded, divinely unfolded, and divinely sustained, in my belief, can never be dissolved. The ends of the world will come upon it, and the light of the Second Advent will find it as it is; and that for this reason: no human hand founded it, and no human hand can overthrow it. No human hand piled the mountains, and no human hand can unpile them; so no hand of man established and interwove the spiritual and temporal sovereignty of the Vicar of Jesus Christ upon earth, and no hand but that which established it can dissolve it. And I believe that hand will not dissolve it, for it was the hand of God Himself; and as the hand of God Himself committed, by His direct providence, to His Vicar upon earth this sovereign rule over the state he holds, so no other hand can revoke His act, can rescind His will, or can abolish His work. No power can conquer it, or acquire it, or possess it. No one can ever obtain a right to that which God has given to His Vicar upon earth. There is an exclusive and expulsive right in the person of His Vicar to that territory over which he reigns; and no human law, no human conquest, no human compact, no human revolution, can create a right against God's right, or abolish the right which God Himself made.

For we see that it is the law of the Church of God never to recede in its path. As it was said of the Roman Empire, *Roma nunquam recedit*, "Rome

never goes back," so the Church never recedes. Rome never gathered in its frontiers, never contracted its boundaries. Its legions marched straight onward ; its military roads crossed plains, deserts, mountains, without turning to the right hand or the left. If they encountered a rock, they pierced it. If they reached the foot of a mountain-range, they scaled it. The irresistible persistence, the inflexible direction, the governing will of that great empire, never wavered or retired. It was in the natural order a faint and feeble symbol of the Church of God. The prophet Isaias foretold that the kingdom which should be given to the incarnate Son of God should be " for ever." The prophet Daniel says, it " shall never be destroyed." The Archangel Gabriel foretold that He should " reign in the house of Jacob for ever." *
And the Church, in her creed, prophesies, " of whose kingdom there shall be no end." Such, in a higher order, is the irresistible onward persistency of the Church, unfolding, developing, multiplying its powers and prerogatives, never contracting, never receding, never withering away. *Folium ejus non defluit.* Not a leaf shall float to the ground. It is the tree of life, always putting forth vitality, never contracting its fruitfulness, its stature, or its expanse.

And therefore, as we believe that in the beginning the Church, by its simple, spiritual power,

* St. Luke i. 32.

subdued the world, and then by its twofold power, spiritual and civil, created Christendom, and has called into existence monarchies and kingdoms, and empires and confederations of empires, and has created even the law of nations by which the world is civilised and held together; so also we believe that its great mission shall go onward to the end, and that the Church will be as it has been, and now is, the sole sustaining power of Christendom. They who believe that Christendom was created by the Church must believe that the Church of God shall not cease to sustain it, unless they believe that Christendom will cease to be. And those who believe that Christendom will come to an end have need to square their theory with the words of the Son of God, "Thou art Peter, and upon this rock will I build My Church, and the gates of hell shall not prevail against it."

Then still further we may see in history, that it was the personal sovereignty of the Pontiffs which held together and maintained the local sovereignty committed to them. The earthly possession, which was, as it were, the body to the soul, the earthen vessel of the Divine gift, has been held together and maintained by the supernatural personal rights and prerogatives committed to the Vicar of Jesus Christ.

First of all, they purchased it by a line of martyrdoms. It is the law of warfare that the army which remains upon the field is victor. If the assailant cannot drive it from its entrenchments, or dislodge it from the post which it holds, it remains the conqueror, and it sets up the trophies of victory. Some thirty Pontiffs fell upon the field. By their blood they purchased the city of Rome, and held it as their own. All the power of ten persecutions, and all the legions of Rome, and all the emperors of the world, could not drive out the Pontiffs from the city which they held for the Son of God. It is theirs by conquest, and by the laws of warfare. It belongs to them by right of endurance, and of patience, and of inflexible courage, to which the world has no equal. Memory fails altogether in attempting to recount the long roll of the contest, and the glories of the Vicars of Jesus Christ. After three hundred years of conflict came no true peace, but a mere change of weapons.

Pope Liberius was banished by an heretical emperor.

Silverius died in exile.

Vigilius was imprisoned and exiled.

St. Martin died in exile a martyr.

St. Leo III. was driven out to Spoleto.

Leo V. was dethroned and cast into prison.

John XII. had to fly from Rome.

Benedict V. was carried off into Germany.

John XIII. fled from a Roman faction, and took refuge in Capua.

Benedict VI. was imprisoned and murdered by a Roman faction.

John XIV. was cast into the prison of St. Angelo, and died of hunger.

Gregory V. was compelled to fly from Rome by a civil tumult.

Benedict VIII. was driven from Rome by a faction.

Benedict IX. was twice driven from Rome.

Leo IX. was dethroned by the Normans.

St. Gregory VII. went from land to land and from kingdom to kingdom, and died in exile.

Victor III. could not so much as take possession of his See, and died at Beneventum.

Urban II. was restored by the French crusaders.

Pascal II. was carried off by Henry V. and imprisoned.

Gelasius II. was compelled to fly to Gaeta, which has been again and again glorious as the refuge of the Vicar of Jesus Christ.

Honorius II. was compelled to fly into France by an anti-Pope who usurped his See.

Eugenius III. was driven out of Rome by Arnold of Brescia.

Alexander III., on the very day of his consecration, was cast into prison. He was consecrated, not in the holy city, but in a village church. He was obliged to fly into the mountains for safety. He passed seven years wandering from Terracina to Anagni, from Anagni to Tusculum.

Urban III. and Gregory VIII. could not even take possession of Rome.

Lucius III. fled to Verona.

Gregory IX. was compelled by an insurrection at Rome to retire to Perugia.

Innocent IV. fled to Genoa.

Alexander IV. fled to Viterbo.

Martin IV. never entered Rome.

Boniface VIII. was a prisoner at Anagni.

Then came the great Western schism, which lasted for seventy years, during which time seven Popes reigned in Avignon.

Urban VI. fled to Genoa.

Innocent VII. fled from the factions of Rome to Viterbo.

Gregory XI. fled to Gaeta.

John XXIII. fled from Rome.

Eugenius IV. was besieged in his own palace by an anti-Pope, and was obliged to fly to Florence.

I might add many more, but it is enough to sum them up: thirty were compelled to leave Rome; four were imprisoned; four were unable to set foot in Rome; seven reigned in exile in Avignon; making in all forty-five, or one-fifth in the line of the Sovereign Pontiffs.*

Now, from this I draw two evident conclusions:

* Theologia Wircembergensis, tom. i. pp. 385-395. Kenrick, Theol. Dogm. vol. i. app. 2. La Voie Douloureuse des Papes, app. 2.

first, that sufferings, anxieties, uncertainty, conflicts within and without, have always been, and always will be, the normal condition of the Vicar of Jesus Christ. As a multitude of facts in the physical world form the basis of a philosophical induction, so by these facts in the history of the Pontiffs it is established as a law, that, so to speak, the normal state and habitual condition of the Vicar of Jesus Christ on earth is to live as Jesus lived Himself, in suffering, contradiction, and conflict. The very city and people committed to him have participated in his fortunes. There has hardly been a century when the hand of usurpers and invaders has not been upon the city of Rome. Whether by barbarian hordes, or Arian Lombards, or emperors of Germany, or counts of the Marches or of Tusculum, or factions of the Cenci or the Colonna, Rome has been always coveted and assailed. There has hardly been a century in which the States of the Church have not been occupied, dismembered, and usurped.* Nine Pontiffs were driven out of Rome by the Roman factions. Seven times the city of Rome has been sacked, ruined, desolated, or taken; twice it was all but levelled. Once it was wholly and entirely destroyed: for forty days it was given up to desolation; no creature breathed within its walls.†

---

* Miley's History of the Roman State, *passim*.

† " Post quam (scil. Totilæ) devastationem, xl. aut amplius dies Roma fuit ita desolata, ut nemo ibi hominum nisi bestiæ moraren-

Nine times the city, in which is the throne of the Vicar of Jesus Christ, has been in the hands of usurpers; yet it has been held with such invincible tenacity of endurance, and such perpetual power of recovery, as to establish as a moral certainty that God, who chose it for the throne of the Vicar of His Son, has done so by a definitive act of His power, which He alone can rescind, and which He never will.

The other conclusion is this: in the history of the Holy See, we observe likewise, that as the normal state and condition of the Supreme Pontiff is to live in perpetual conflict, and as it is the law, so to speak, of the temporal sovereignty committed to him that it should be perpetually assailed, so there is another law equally certain, founded on the same basis, and established by the same induction, namely, that it is also his normal condition to be always restored. This law of restoration is founded upon and deduced from the same series of facts, and from the same evidence. As often as his sovereignty has been usurped, so often has it been restored to him; and as it has been, so it will be to the end. And what, above all, is remarkable is this, that the hands used to restore him have often been the most unlikely to do this service. They have, indeed, been sometimes Catholic kings, like Pepin and Charlemagne; but at

tur." Marcell. in Chron. ad annum A.D. 547. Biblioth. Max. Gallandii, tom. x. p. 356.

other times the same hands which drove him from Rome have restored him to it. Again, sometimes the very mob of Rome have come out in procession to recall their pastors; at other times, those who have been interested in resisting his return, as the English nation and the Russian schismatics, have restored him. Again and again those who, in the hands of Almighty God, have sustained the temporal sovereignty have been those who, judging by what the world calls reasonable and politic, for their own interest would have most opposed it; that all mankind may see that God rules the world.

The conclusion, then, I wish to establish is this, that the last glories of the Holy See will be greater than the first; for its imperishable vitality and divine tenacity of endurance has been, and ever will be, more and more luminously manifested in the struggle through which it is passing. It will be more clearly seen by all the world that the sole principle of stability to be found among men is the Church Catholic and Roman; that all forms of human institution are transitory, dissolving, and self-destructive. The Roman State has been changed and fashioned again and again into counties and duchies, into kingdoms and provinces of empires. Where, I should like to know, at this moment is the very name of those kingdoms and of their lords who claimed to be its temporal governors? Where now is Napoleon, "King of Rome"? And where to-morrow will be Victor Emmanuel, "King of Italy"? All these occasional forms of rebellion, revolution, and disorder, which spring from the will of man, have a momentary success, and in a little while are not. God, with a divine scorn and with a majestic indignation, smites them as small as the dust of the summer threshing-floor, and the winds of His derision sweep them from the face of the earth.

But the Church of God is divine, and the principles of the Church of God are His revelation and His providence—His revealed will and His Divine action. The Church of God has no need to recast and recreate itself. It never changes its character; it never puts off its old form for new combinations. It was never otherwise than it is; and what it is, it ever shall be. The Pontiff, who now reigns from the Apostolic See over the Universal Church of God, stands alone firm and changeless in the mutations and instability of all around. He answers, as his predecessors have answered before him, "*Non volumus, non possumus, non debemus*"—"We will not, we cannot, we ought not." In those three words Pius VII. refused to make cession of one jot or tittle of the right which God had given to him. He held them not for himself alone—he held them for God and for the Church: not as owner and lord, but as trustee and steward. What was not his own, he could not give away. That which God had entrusted to him, God would require of him. Therefore he would not, could not, ought not to yield, come what might. He appealed to the Divine providence of God, and the hand of God scattered his antagonists. In a little while the Vicar of Jesus Christ was found once more reigning upon his throne, tranquil and sovereign as before.

In like manner in our day Pius IX. has refused, with a constancy and a steadfastness which this proud world calls obstinacy and stubbornness, to make concession or compromise. In like manner he has appealed to the providence of God, and his appeal has gone up to heaven. When the prophet Elias appealed to the God of Israel, the priests of Baal cut themselves with knives, and leaped upon the altar; so now the Priest and Prophet of the Christian law, standing by the tomb of the Apostles, has appealed to God, and his voice has gone up on high. As yet there is silence in heaven. "There is no voice, and none to answer." The world is full of triumphant joy at its success, so near to come. But there is more power in the aged man who stands upon the tomb of the Apostles, and lifts the Holy Sacrifice to the four quarters of the world which it has redeemed, than in the pride of life, and the vigour of intellect, and the strong tide of blood and will which direct the nations against him.

The other day it seemed an unequal contest; he in his lonely weakness, right alone on his side, all might against him. Cunning, and diplomacy, and the confederate interests of kingdoms and states—all against him in array. It was but a week ago when this manifold power was wielded by a hand * thought to be so unerring that the men of this world for the last three days have been telling us that a great light has gone out in the world. Whether the voice has come in answer, I know not. The Church of God does not pursue its antagonists beyond the grave. The sacred procession bearing the last Sacraments goes to the dwelling of the rich man as well as of the poor, of the disobedient as well as of the faithful. It seeks out the dying penitent, whether it be a poor daughter fallen as Mary Magdalene, or a proud son who lifted up his heel against the Church of God.

Of the future we know nothing; into the unseen world we cannot enter. But of one thing I am sure. For the last three days there is no man who believes in the providence of God, no man who has read the history of the last twelve years, but has felt with a silent fear that there is a Will above all human wills directing this great conflict. The prophet Daniel tells us that in the latter days the God of Heaven shall set up a kingdom; and he adds, *Regnum ejus*

* Count Cavour.

alteri populo non tradetur,—" His kingdom shall not be delivered over to another people."* No other shall ever possess it; no other shall ever conquer it; but it will break to pieces, and it will destroy all other kingdoms,—*Sed ipsum stabit in æternum,*— " but it shall stand for ever."

* Daniel ii. 44.

LECTURE II.

"Ought not Christ to have suffered these things, and so to enter into His glory?"—St. Luke xxiv. 26.

EVEN the loving and faithful hearts of the disciples were so amazed and darkened by the Passion of Jesus, that they knew not that His kingdom was accomplishing itself. When they looked for the splendour and the majesty of His power, they met with His humiliations and His Cross; and therefore they did not know Him when He manifested Himself to them. They looked for Him in one form, and He showed Himself in another. They said, "We hoped that it was He that should have redeemed Israel," and now behold He is crucified, and even the place of His burial is empty. And our Divine Lord answered them, "O foolish, and slow of heart to believe in all things which the prophets have spoken. Ought not Christ to have suffered these things?" Was there not a law of necessity? Was it not predestinated? Was it not foretold? Was there not intrinsic fitness that Christ should suffer these things, "and so,"—by this way, and by no other, by the way of suffering, and not by the way of glory,—should enter into His kingdom?

This, then, is the sum of what I have already said. The Church of God, being united to its Head, partakes of the same destinies in time and in eternity, on earth and in heaven. The Church on earth shares in the Passion of the Son of God. The Apostle says that he was filling up "those things that are wanting of the sufferings of Christ"* in the flesh for His Body, which is the Church. And the sufferings which are to be accomplished upon earth through the whole mystical body of Christ fall eminently, I will not say exclusively, but fall emphatically, upon its Head, upon the line of the Sovereign Pontiffs. You will remember that we have already seen how the whole history of the Pontiffs upon earth has been a history of suffering, of anxiety, and of conflict; how by perpetual usurpation and perpetual oppression the people over whom they reign have been divided and harassed, the territory they possess occupied and ravaged; and how, by a series of perpetual restorations, the hand of God has intervened to re-establish the order which He Himself created. In His kingdom there is a perpetuity, not only in its spiritual elements, but in all those complex forms of power which He, by direct and indirect operation, has woven together. The whole sovereignty of the Church, spiritual and temporal, as it is at this hour, is the work of God, and, being the work of God, it cannot be destroyed.

* Col. i. 24.

The point, then, which I now wish to bring before you is this—how difficult it is for us to appreciate the times in which we live. Our belief must be that, according to the analogy of all God's dealings, the last glories of His Church on earth will be greater than the first. And yet perhaps we are perplexed to understand how this can be verified. We look at the present state of the Church in the world, and all seems dark before us. The reason is this, that it is difficult for us justly to estimate and to understand the days in which we are. As we cannot measure the motion by which we are carried along, as no man, perhaps, knows his own countenance, or is conscious of his own stature, so it is with the times that are upon us. The evils fill the whole field of our vision. They seem so vast and so overwhelming, and that which is good so scarce and hardly to be found; for the evils are present in power, but the good is generally in germ and for the future. It is necessary, therefore, that the present should be known by retrospect. And the greatest times and the most glorious are often those which look darkest when they are near. The days, therefore, which are upon us now, though heavy shadows and dark clouds hang upon the horizon, will doubtless hereafter be glorious to those who see them afar off; and I may say without rashness that they will be more glorious than any times we read of in the history of the Church.

In order to show this, I wish to examine, as shortly as I can, certain other periods of history which we look upon now as periods of especial glory, and to show that they were moments which those who lived in them looked upon as times of the greatest darkness, suffering, and tribulation, pregnant with evils known and unknown for the present and the future.

1. First of all, look to the times of the first and great St. Gregory, to whom the name of Great attaches, because in his own person he seemed to sum up the glories of the Church on earth. First, he was a saint, shining with the resplendent lustre of a singular sanctity, a sun in the firmament of the Church. Next, he was a doctor, the last of the four great lights, to whom the Church has added no more of a like splendour. There are four Gospels, and there are four doctors—four lights which stand at the four corners of the Church. He was also the apostle of nations; England owes its Christianity to him; and all of the Anglo-Saxon race that remain faithful to the Holy See at this day throughout the world are the sons and daughters of St. Gregory the Great. Lastly, he was a patriarch, reigning by an especial parental sway, whereby he ruled the three-and-twenty patrimonies of the Holy See with an authority so benign and sweet, so full of evangelical prudence and of the Spirit of God, that he moulded to his will the hearts of men, and by love and the law of Jesus laid

the foundations of the Christian order which overspreads the world. We look back, then, on the times of St. Gregory as times of especial glory.

But what were they in reality? Rome was desolated by pestilence; for seven months the Holy See was vacant;* Pelagius, the last Pontiff, died of the plague; processions that went about the streets were so ravaged by it, that, in the midst of the sacred ceremonial, and in one alone, eighty men fell dead. In such a moment it was, when Rome was plague-stricken and desolate, that St. Gregory ascended the throne of the Apostle. And when he looked around him, what met his sight? Was the Christian world as we behold it at this time? In the East, once full of the light of faith, the great Oriental churches of Asia were ravaged by two dominant heresies, the Eutychian and the Nestorian. Their poison had spread even into China. Already the spirit of schism had possessed itself of Constantinople, and the emperors of the East had become forerunners of the imperial Antichrists of the Middle Ages. The patriarchs of Constantinople had begun to assume the arrogant title which St. Gregory denounced as the usurpation of Antichrist. Russia did not exist. Norway and Sweden were hardly known among the nations. Heathenism covered them all. Spain was

* Bolland. Acta Sanctorum, 12 die Martii. Palma, Prælect. Hist. Eccl. c. lxvi.

Arian, and persecuted the Catholic Church. England had relapsed into Paganism; the light of faith had gone out; the heathenism of the Saxons and the Danes reigned over it. Lombardy was Arian, and the Lombards ravaged Italy up to the walls of Rome.

Such was the world over which St. Gregory reigned and sorrowed. His life, like that of Jeremias the prophet, was a ceaseless lamentation. Any one who reads his letters, and his expositions of the Holy Scriptures, will find perpetual strains of mourning over the desolation of Rome and the death of the world. He says: "Rome is ravaged; its very structure is dissolved. Not its glory alone, but its life is departed. We die daily. Sorrow and grief are on every side. We are pursuing after the world, and the world is departing from us. We cleave to it, and it passes away."* He believed that the end of all things had come. Such in his eyes were the times of which, seen in the unclouded light of history, the glory is to us so great and splendid.

2. Let us pass onward some two hundred years, and then comes another period of Christian grandeur, the age of St. Leo III.; of whom we conceive that he must have been majestic and mighty indeed, who could create an emperor and an empire—an empire pregnant with modern Europe. And what must have

* Hom. in Festo SS. Nerei et Achillei.

been the tree which cast such a seed containing the stateliness of a forest? We cannot but imagine to ourselves how vast must have been the power of such a Pontiff, and how splendid, and out of all proportion to these later times, must have been the age in which he lived. But how was it in truth?

St. Leo lived in an age when Mahometanism had already possessed itself of the three great Eastern Patriarchates: Jerusalem, Antioch, and Alexandria were in the hands of the false prophet. The Eastern Churches had fallen under the darkness of the infidel. Northern Africa was entirely swept by it. Five hundred episcopal sees, it is said, were wholly overthrown. The Churches of St. Cyprian, and St. Augustine, and St. Optatus were held by the Eastern Antichrist. Mahometanism had penetrated into Spain; it had come up by the south, and was encompassing Christendom. The Paganism of Germany had broken over the Rhine, and entered into France.* Lombardy was still usurping the patrimony of the Church, and civil factions were in Rome itself. St. Leo was assaulted in the midst of a sacred procession, when, on St. George's day, he was going from St. Lorenzo in Lucina to St. George in Velabro, by a band of assassins.† They fell upon him, and stripped him of his pontifical robes; they wounded him, and dragged

---

* Ranke, Hist. of the Popes, book i. c. i. s. 2.
† Bolland. Acta Sanctorum, 12 die Junii.

him violently to prison. Such were the times in which he lived, and such was the cause in which he invoked the aid of Charlemagne, on whose brow on the day of the Nativity he set the diadem of empire. We picture Charlemagne standing in St Peter's, over the tomb of the Apostle, arrayed in imperial robes, and St. Leo, a greater than he, standing by his side, the Sovereign Pontiff and Vicar of Jesus Christ, bestowing upon him the diadem of the world in the midst of a court of splendour and majesty, such as we have seen in these days of power and peace. It was in the midst of no such Christmas solemnities, but of humiliation and tumult and personal assault, that this great act of the Christian world was done. The days were darker far than ours, when the great Head of the Faithful cast the seed of a new order, and the foundations of our Christendom were laid.

3. Let us, then, take another period—that of St. Gregory VII.—some two or three hundred years later. We picture him to ourselves as historians—especially those who are without the light of faith—are always fond of drawing him, in the majesty and elevation of his sovereign power, reposing in the fortress of Canossa, while an Emperor of Germany waited outside the gate, in the snows of the Apennines, all the night long, till the Pontiff was pleased to absolve him from the censures of the Church. We imagine that St. Gregory was then at the pitch of

greatness and the plenitude of power, and wielded unbounded sway over the Church of God and the nations of the world. But those times were times of conflict greater than any that had gone before. At the very moment when he ascended the throne of the Apostles, the Church was, in every part of Europe, groaning under the oppression of the civil powers. Two hundred years had passed since that Christmas-day in which St. Leo had created the empire. Monarchies and states had arisen in Western Europe. In every one of them those who ruled in the civil order had become the oppressors of the Church. In every place they usurped ecclesiastical power, and contended with the Holy See. The territories of the Ecclesiastical State were in such a condition, that I can only describe it in St. Gregory's own words. In a letter to the Abbot of Clugni, of which monastery he had been a monk, he says:

"*Gregory, Bishop, servant of the servants of God, to Hugh, Abbot of Clugni, health and apostolic benediction.*

"If it can be, I desire that you should fully know how great a sorrow presses upon me, and how great a burden, renewed day by day, weighs me down; that your brotherly compassion may incline towards me, and that your heart and your tears may be poured out before God in prayer, that Jesus, who was made poor for us, through whom all things were made, and who rules all things, may stretch forth His hand, and with His wonted kindness deliver me from my misery. For I have often asked Him, as He enables me, either to take me out of this present life, or to make me useful to our common Mother: nevertheless He has not set me free from this great anguish, neither has my life profited the Church, in the bonds of which He has bound me. For an overwhelming grief and an universal sorrow surround me on every side. The Eastern Church, by the instinct of the devil, has revolted from the Catholic Faith, and in its members the old enemy is everywhere putting Christians to death. When I look to the West, or South, or North, I can hardly see a Bishop, who by his entrance on the Episcopate, or by his life, is such as the Canons demand: ruling the Christian people for the love of Christ, and not for worldly ambition; and among all the secular princes, not one who prefers the honour of God to his own, or justice to gain, do I know. As for the people among whom I live,—I mean the Romans, Lombards, and Normans,—as I am often telling them, they are in a way worse than Jews and Pagans." *

On his ascending the Apostolic Throne, he found three great evils laying waste the Church. The first was immorality and simony in the highest places;

* Epist. S. Greg. VII., lib. ii. ep. iv., ed. Migne.

the next was the supremacy of the temporal power over the spiritual; and the third—far more penetrating, and far more subtle—was the claim of the civil powers to give investiture even to spiritual offices by the ring and crosier; that is, in fact, to claim to themselves to be the fountain of authority over the Church of God. As soon as he set his foot upon the throne, he issued his decrees of burning indignation; and in the moment those decrees were issued, they were met on all sides by opposition. Writing to our own Archbishop Lanfranc of Canterbury, he says, "To escape the judgments of God, I must encounter a host of enemies, and bring them down upon myself."*

His decrees of reformation were met in France by such refusal that all the Bishops of the kingdom except two failed in their fidelity. These two were Rouen and Poictiers, on which an hereditary grace seems still to rest. He wrote to the Bishops of France in these words:

"If in this great and necessary duty we find you to be lukewarm, we at once, having no more doubt that the king, supported by confidence in you, persists incorrigibly, shall smite you, as the companions and accomplices in his sin, with an equal punishment, and shall strip you of the episcopal office."†

* Epist. S. Greg. VII., pars ii. ep. i.
† Ibid. ad Episcopos Francorum, lib. ii. ep. v., ed. Migne.

In England, in the Council of Winchester, the Archbishop stood alone. In Germany, the Archbishop of Metz temporised. In Spain, the papal legate was insulted. In Rome, the simoniacal prelates, being suspended, immediately joined the factions of the nobles. Then began the contest. The whole life of Gregory was a life of warfare; not a pause or a truce till death. On the night of Christmas he had just celebrated the first Mass of the Nativity, and distributed the precious Body and Blood of Jesus to those about him, when an armed faction broke into the church, dragged him from the altar, rent from him his pontifical vestments, even the vestments of the Holy Sacrifice, wounded him with a sword upon the head, and bore him away to prison. Such were the first fruits of his fidelity to his Divine Master. After this, in exile he wandered to and fro, and ended at last a long life of supernatural sorrow at Salerno, saying, "I have loved justice and hated iniquity, and therefore I die in exile."* Such was the great St. Gregory VII., on whom we look back as the most glorious of the Pontiffs of the Middle Ages. His days were days of darkness, and clouds and storms surrounded him. Many men about him believed, or feared, at least, that he was, if not on the losing side, at least doomed to suffer almost in vain. We look back upon him

* Voigt, Hist. du Pape Grég. VII., liv. vi. vol. xii.

now as the great Pontiff who subdued the empire, and cleansed the sanctuary of the Church.

4. Then, to come down a little later, let us take the period of Alexander III., who is described to us in history riding upon his palfry with a king of France and a king of England on either side; or as in conference with the emperor at Venice, and receiving by his full concession an acknowledgment of the great prerogatives for which St. Gregory VII. had contended and suffered. We invest Alexander III. with an excess of majesty, with all the attributes of pontifical splendour, and suppose him to have been head of all the powers of the world, and his days to be times of empire, not of conflict.

And yet, what is the truth?

As soon as he was elected, an anti-Pope was created by the emperor. The same power caused him to be imprisoned on the very day of his election. He could not be consecrated with the solemnities usual to the Pontiffs, but he was consecrated in a parish church. He was compelled to leave the city of Rome and take refuge at Terracina, and Anagni, and Tusculum. Thenceforth, for seven years, he wandered to and fro; his life was spent in solitary conflict with all the powers of the world arrayed against him. At that time Mahometanism had long swept all round the south, and reigned in Spain. It seemed as if the power of Antichrist were on the point of destroying Christendom. The schism of the East had long accomplished itself. Constantinople was finally separated from the Holy See; the four Eastern Patriarchates were under the dominion of schism or of Mahometanism. Italy was ravaged by the German emperor, who aimed at establishing the old Roman empire on the basis of its ancient imperial laws. Rome was divided into two contending parties—the nobles and the emperor striving to enslave the Church, the Pontiff and the people vindicating the freedom and sovereignty of Jesus Christ. It is the old contest, the Pontifex Maximus of heathen Rome against the Supreme Pontiff, Vicar of Jesus. The civil society of Italy was full of factions perpetually contending. There was the faction of the seditious in Rome, stimulated by foreign influence, and by the imperial partisans, aiming at the kingdom of Italy. And there was but one obstacle in the way, and that one obstacle was then in the 12th century the same as in the 19th still. Rome alone stood in his path;* not because Rome is strong, for its walls would crumble before the first stroke of war, but because Rome is a Divine foundation, and is the centre of Divine principles and the source of Divine power. Because Rome is the head of the Church of God, and because Rome controls the consciences, the hearts, the wills of men and nations, therefore

* Ranke, Hist. of the Reformation, Introd. p. 57.

it is that Rome belongs not to the Romans, but to the Christians. Christendom will not receive a pagan empire; and the Pontiff of the Church of God is strong, because he represents the sovereignty of the Son of God and of the whole mystical body of the Son of God, which refuses to be subject to the world. The contest was the same then as now, and will be to the end.

5. The last period which I shall take is that of Clement VII. We come then nearer to our own times. The splendour of the Pontificate for the last three hundred years so fills our minds, that we conceive perhaps, that in the time of the so-called Reformation the power and the majesty of the Holy See was not overcast, as it is in our days. But what is the truth? First of all, by that time Mahometanism had not only possessed itself of Constantinople, but penetrated almost to the walls of Vienna. The Turks hung upon Christendom; so that for eighty years to come it seemed as if they were about to extinguish the light of Christianity. The shores of Italy and the Patrimony of the Church were harassed by them. You all remember how the great St. Pius V. afterwards accomplished by his prayers the last overthrow of the Eastern Antichrist. Down to that time, the perils, the hovering assaults of Mahometanism on Christianity, were perpetually drawing nearer and nearer. The nations of Europe, grown

proud in their nationality by two hundred years of schism, sometimes perfectly accomplished, and always threatened, were jealous and full of disobedience to the Holy See. In England, Henry VIII. perpetrated the first act of separation in the time of Clement VII. Luther had begun to spread his heresy. It had penetrated throughout Germany into Switzerland and England, and partially into France and Spain. The condition of Italy seemed hopeless. The emperors of Germany sent an army against the city of Rome to besiege the Father of the Faithful; and at that moment the factions of Rome, headed by the Colonna, one of the chief families, by force of arms drove the Pope into the Castle of St. Angelo, and assumed the government of the city. In this state the Pope was reduced to the last condition of distress, at a time when we think he was in the zenith of power. The army of the emperor came onward, breathing threats and slaughter against the disciples of Jesus Christ. I use the words advisedly; for we read that a German noble, one of the leaders on the march, said, "If I go to Rome, I will take the Pontiff's life," in language which, for its vileness, I will not speak. But God had marked him for his fate.* He never set foot in Rome, for apoplexy struck him down by the way. The Constable of Bourbon, on the scaling-

* Ranke, Hist. of the Popes, b. i. c. 3.

ladder which he had placed against the walls, was likewise struck down. The city was for nine months sacked and pillaged, and we are told by historians of every kind, Catholic and un-Catholic, that Rome never suffered, under Goths, Vandals, or Lombards, humiliations or horrors equalling those of that siege. No state, no age, no condition, no sex was spared in the horrors of that time. And this befell in the time of the Reformation, when Mahometanism was at its greatest power, when the heresy of Luther was already dominant in the greater part of Northern Europe. Italy was almost entirely in the hands of the secular power. Rome itself was desolate. What could be darker than this? And yet this was the time when the preludes of the great Council of Trent were preparing; the first preparations were being made for that Great Synod which has given to the Pontificate and to the Church of God a splendour and a sway, not only by authority and discipline, but by the persuasions of love, of conviction, and of reason, which exceed all that the world has ever seen before.

I can do no more than touch on these five periods of darkness, which we look on as periods of surpassing glory. And periods of glory they were, glory greater than we can conceive; for we do not know, and never shall till we read history with the interpretation and light of the future, how divine was the power of the Holy See in those great contests.

From all this I draw certain plain truths. First of all, that those times were dark beyond anything we see now. They were times of old heresies and of new. They were times when arose the greatest heresy that has ever afflicted the Church of God—I mean that which is now upon it; for there has been none so widespread, none so manifold, none so hostile, none so universal in its denial of the revelation of God. They were ages in which there were also schisms both old and new; when the far East separated itself, and the Eastern Patriarchates fell away. They were the ages when Mahomet appeared, when the great Eastern Antichrist arose and nearly possessed himself of the world. They were ages when the secular power arose against the Church of God, and intruded itself into the whole life and action of the ecclesiastical order, with an oppression which now is matter of history; for we find it nowhere except lingering in some Protestant countries, and chiefly in England. It was the age, too, when the States of the Holy See were again and again in the possession of usurpers. During those five periods they were perpetually ravaged and harassed by Lombards, or Hungarians, or emperors of Germany, or by factions of the nobles of the Marches or of Rome.

What could be darker than these epochs of the

past? Yet we look back upon them now as the most bright and glorious times in the annals of the Church.

Let me draw but one conclusion more. If these days are times of trial to the Church of God on earth; if the Holy See itself be circumvented and threatened now; and if the fidelity of Christian nations shows itself to be unstable,—what is there in this that we have not seen before, and seen even exceeded, I may say, a thousand times? Never, until now, was the power of the Church of God so widely spread; nor did it ever so occupy the four quarters of the world, and penetrate among all heathen races, and possess itself so nearly of the circuit of mankind. Never was there a time when the Pontificate of the successor of St. Peter was more ample, more universally recognised and loved, or more firmly upheld by the prayers and hearts of the whole Christian world. Never was there a time when the Pontificate was illustrated by such acts of apostolic power, the creation of new hierarchies, and the definition of the glory of our Immaculate Mother. Never was there a time when the firmness of the Holy See was more commanding, or the person of the Holy Father, even in the eyes of the world, more spotless. We have reason to be ashamed of every man who has engaged in this contest against the Church of God. Emperors and kings, princes and statesmen, alike, every one who has moved either tongue or hand against the Holy See, has soiled and shamed himself. But the Sovereign Pontiff stands in light without a cloud. I might ask, what is there in the Pontificate that is not great—that will not be glorious hereafter? But on this I will not dwell. I will sum up all in one principle: that which appears to be weak in the present, is charged with victory hereafter.

The period of St. Gregory I. was an epoch of apostolical power in the conversion of nations.

The period of St. Leo III. was an epoch of creation, and Christian Europe arose in it.

The period of St. Gregory VII. was an epoch of purification, which reached the very inmost life of the Church of God.

The period of Alexander III. was an epoch of supremacy over the powers of the world, which had usurped upon the powers of the Church.

The period of Clement VII. was an epoch when the Pontificate of Jesus Christ, in the person of His Vicar, was more than ever unfolded and made resplendent before the eyes of men. It is a glory which stands steadfast to this day, the light of which flows down upon us even to this hour.

And therefore we may believe that the period in which we live shall have a future. I see that those periods have accumulated one upon another, so that the glories of the first live in the second, the second in the third, the third in the fourth, and so on. All the antecedent glories we find full upon it still. I see, too, another law,—that these glories rise, increase, and culminate. They are always growing ampler as time goes on. And in this we have a law laid down, namely, that the future shall be more glorious than the past, and that the last glories of the Holy See shall be greater than the first. You know that the revolution—that is, the rising of men without God, united to dethrone the Vicar of Jesus Christ—is increasing, multiplying, enlarging itself throughout Europe. It is coming down from the north as Mahometanism came up by the south—spreading along the whole line, and encompassing the north of Christendom as Mahometanism enclosed the south. But as Mahometanism had its battle of Lepanto, so certainly will the revolution directed against the Vicar of Jesus Christ have its overthrow. When, in what way, where, or by whom, I know not; but so it will be. And the Church of God will remain immovable among the ruins. And this confidence is founded, not upon human history, nor upon the opinions of men. The power of God, which launched the planets in the impetuosity of their career, controls them also by another law of wisdom, and guides them perpetually in their unerring path. They would fall off into infinite space, if they were not held in the sweet control of perpetual order, which manifests the glory and the wisdom of God. The impetuosity of man would ravage the earth, if there were not a higher will above to control its action. Over the will of man is the will of God. "The Gentiles raged, and the people devised vain things. The kings of the earth stood up, and the princes met together against the Lord and against His Christ." * But there is a will above them all, prescribing their path. They cannot swerve to the right hand or to the left. God is above them all. His predestinations are eternal, and the time will come when He will accomplish them. This is our confidence,—a confidence in truths and in principles which are immutable by virtue of their own intrinsic certainty; they must be when the time is come. They cannot fail, for they are divine. "Heaven and earth shall pass away, but My word shall not pass away." †

* Ps. ii. 1, 2.   † St. Mark xiii. 31.

LECTURE III.

"Therefore, receiving an immovable kingdom, we have grace: by which let us serve, pleasing God, with fear and reverence."—HEBREWS xii. 28.

ONE point still remains to complete the subject we have in hand.

I have hitherto endeavoured to show that the glories of the Holy See have continually waxed greater and greater, and shall grow still more resplendent even to the end.

We have already traced this law of increase through the great epochs of its history; and I broke off in speaking of the present times in which we live. It was too large a subject to speak of by the way: it demands a separate treatment. This I will endeavour now to give. But, as I have said before, I am conscious how difficult it is to estimate the times in which we are. All that I can do, therefore, will be to point out some of the signs already visible, and some of the truths and principles already in operation, which give promise of the greater glory yet to come.

We have also seen, that the kingdom of God on earth, being divinely founded, built up, compacted together, and invested with supernatural prerogatives, has a coherence and an indissoluble constitution which no powers of man shall ever destroy. God alone, who created it, has control over its destinies. Wherefore that of which we have heard so much of late from the proud or timid voices of men—the dissolution of the temporal power of the Sovereign Pontiff—is to man an impossibility. God has knit the two persons in a sacred union; and what God has joined together, no man shall put asunder.

We have seen that it is a law of the very being of the Church never to recede from its perfection, but always to press onward, amplifying, unfolding, expanding, filling up, and perfecting that which was before in germ. We have seen that the glories of the Church of God accumulate one upon another. As the splendours of the morning continually increase until they reach their fulness in the noonday; so are the glories of the Church. They do not rise and pass away as the stars of night, but gather, and stand still in multitude and brightness for ever.

And, lastly, we have seen that the glories, prerogatives, and powers of the Church have not only gone on increasing from age to age, but that they have risen by a continual ascent and culmination towards some point not yet attained. What that zenith shall be, God alone, who has predestinated the perfection of the Church, can reveal.

Now what I wish further to point out is, how this law of increase, accumulation, and ascent is to be verified in what is before our eyes at this day.

First of all, there never was an age when the Church was so widely spread over the whole face of the earth. There never was a time when the holy Catholic and Roman Church had so nearly attained the whole circumference of the families of mankind. In the early ages it was an isolated body in the great empire of Rome. Later, it seemed to be shut up in Europe, for the East had fallen into schism and heresy. Then again it pushed out its missions. The sons of St. Dominic and St. Francis penetrated into Palestine and Arabia, and laid the foundations of new churches in the solitudes of the East. Later again, the sons of St. Ignatius penetrated into the West, when a New World was opened to the Old, and there laid the foundations of the Christian order, which endures to this day. But all this was partial, compared with the extension of the Church at this hour. The whole of the vast continent of America, from north to south, is now overspread by the episcopate. The Church possesses the New World for its inheritance, and both worlds for its possession. It has returned again into the East. It is spreading throughout India. It has now once more entered into China; a host of martyrdoms illustrate its advent.*

---

* See the *New Glories of the Catholic Church*, published at Rome by command of the Holy Father Pius IX.

So that at this moment, both in the East and in the West, the Holy See is spreading forth its sway beyond all former expansion. Nay, more than this, it has passed over into the Southern Archipelago. In islands, of which the very names were unknown to it in ages past, the Catholic Church has now its episcopal sees. In one of them alone there is a region as widespread as the whole of Europe. There was a time when the Church in Europe was as infant and narrow in its extent as the Church in Australia now. Who can foretell its future? Who can foresee the order and majesty of the Christendom of the Southern world, which may be now rising to renew and to multiply the glories of the kingdom and the Vicar of Jesus Christ? There was never, therefore, a time when the Church of God had amplified its boundaries, stretched forth its prerogatives, and lifted up its staff of pontifical rule over the face of the earth with so wide-spreading an empire as at this moment. Nay, more; the great empire of Britain, which is more like the ancient Roman than any other, save only that it greatly exceeds it in extent, is, as it were, the beast of burden on which the Church of God has traversed the world. Just as the empire of Rome, in ancient times, fought against the Church, and yet served it, strove to extinguish it, and yet gave it facilities for conquering the world,—so the great empire of Britain, with all its power and civil order and government and enterprise, is assisting, against its own will, and even without its own knowledge, the world-wide operations of the Holy See. This, then, is the first glory of these latter days.

The second is this, that the internal order and spiritual industry of the Church has continually multiplied its operations, distributing itself into new forms and inventions of charity, to an extent never seen before. The great orders of antiquity stand like the stately trees of tropical climates, majestic and fruitful, casting their seeds upon the soil below. Under their shelter, the orders and congregations of active charity in these latter days have sprung up, like the grass which clothes the face of the soil, and overspreads the whole earth with its verdure. It would be impossible to describe or to enumerate the multitude of these new creations of the Holy Spirit. The last three hundred years has teemed with them. Every age has brought forth some new family of charity: Every country has borne its fruit. But chiefly Spain, Italy, and even poor Ireland. In France alone, I believe I may say, there have been founded in the last three centuries no less than a hundred congregations, having each of them a multitude of separate houses spreading all over the land, and numbering thousands and tens of thousands of men and women consecrated to works of charity. And this spreads also over the whole world, for they have offshoots in every land,—in the colonies of Great Britain, in the whole length and breadth of America, among heathen people. There is no part of the world where the tender, delicate, yet daring charity of the daughters of the Church has not penetrated. Never was there a time when the Church of God applied the ministrations of its mercy to the wounds of mankind, spiritual and corporal, with the assiduity that it does at this time. This, too, is a special feature of these latter days.

Then, again, we see a singular industry in the legislation of the Church. The great Council of Trent, which closed three hundred years ago, I may paradoxically say, is sitting to this hour; for its doctrines and discipline rule supreme, and are exerting themselves in every place. The faithful in all lands cherish it as the reformation of the world. It has inscribed itself even in the statute law of kingdoms. The legislation of that great synod, held through times of trouble and suffering for twenty long years, with manifold interruptions, is the living charter of the Church, ruling at this day throughout the world. It has also set in motion the councils and synods of provinces and dioceses in the East and West; so that I may say that this century also, like the century which followed immediately upon the Council of Trent, is a century of ecclesiastical legislation—then, to carry out its decrees, now, to apply them to the new conditions of society.

Next comes a third and singular phenomenon, which is, that the principle of heresy seems to be smitten with its death-blow. I do not say of error, nor of ignorance, nor of indifference, nor of infidelity; for there is too much of all these, and no doubt there always will be; but the principle of heresy properly so called,—the proud, contentious, private spirit among those who profess themselves Christians, by which they erect themselves against the authority of the Church of God. Perhaps this may seem to be incredible with Protestantism before us. But even Protestantism itself is now no more a religion. In the first forty years after it arose, it spread itself, to and fro, among some of the northern countries of Europe; after that it made no further progress. It never advanced anywhere. It was a political religion, forced on the people by legislatures and by princes. It did not spring up from the multitude like the apostolic missions; it came from the civil power, embodied in statute laws, enforced by penalties. And when the enforcement of penalties ceased, the religion ceased to spread. The present state of Protestant countries will show that it has no propagation as a religion, no definiteness, consistency, or permanence; it has been continually dividing and dissolving, until it has sunk down in the countries which gave it birth into a simple unbelief.

Rationalism, ignorance, indifference, and infidelity, the four evils of which we have too plentiful a harvest, are the direct result and consequence of the principles of Protestantism. The offspring live on, but the parent is death-struck. Where, then, is heresy? The old are long since gone. Who ever hears now of Arianism, or Nestorianism, or Pelagianism? And just as they are extinct already, so will Protestantism, as a religion, be extinct hereafter; I say as a religion, not as a political system, not as a principle of political revolution. In this form it lives, and will live on in the world. But as a religion, as a form of doctrine, as a form of interpreting the Holy Scriptures, where is it already? It has dispersed, and has taken endless forms of change. And where is there a heresy rising up to replace it? No one will call Mormonism a heresy; nor the eclectic imitation of the Catholic Church which has shown itself among individuals in Scotland and in England. These are mere aberrations of the human mind. There is nothing permanent, or solid, or logical in them; nothing that can give an account of itself, bad or unfounded as that account may be. For eighteen hundred years the contest has been going on, and the world is weary of it. Men say, 'if there be a Church on earth, it is the Catholic and Roman; if there be dogma, it is the faith of the Council of Trent. Fragmentary religions have been tried, and found wanting. Human teachers are blind guides, and human opinions have no certainty. If there be a revelation, it must be divinely certain; and to be divinely certain, we need a Divine Witness and a Divine Teacher. Everything has deceived and betrayed us. New religions are self-condemned.' It seems as if the winds and the waves had been rebuked, and that a great calm has fallen upon the world. It is the age of the Immaculate Conception; and the peace of the world is a fulfilment of that prophetic antiphon of the Church, "Tu sola cunctas hæreses interemisti in universo mundo." It pleased God not only to reveal the singular privilege of His Immaculate Mother, but also to make the definition an occasion of manifesting His infallibility in the midst of a weary and contentious world.

The Faith is now standing out with a singular prerogative. It is the sole and only immutable religion known to men. What we call truths, the world calls errors. But it admits that Rome never changes. The world says that the Catholic doctrines rise from the hearts of men. We know that they come from the revelations of God. In this we differ; but both are agreed in the immutability which sustains the Church of God. Even the world can see that Rome never changes; that her doctrines are always the same. Even the world knows that errors are always changing; that truth alone is immutable. If they will not admit the Catholic faith to be true, they accuse it of immutability; and honest men are drawing the conclusion. If there be anything worn out and cast aside, it is the heresy of private judgment. Men have seen its legitimate consequences in modern infidelity. It is the principle of heresy therefore that stands convicted; and men confess the need, if not the presence, of a Divine Teacher.

And further, there was never a time when the whole world was united with such a close bond of filial charity and docile obedience to the See of Rome as at this. There were periods in the Middle Ages, of which I have spoken before, when the proud nationalities of Europe rose in contention against the Vicar of Jesus Christ. There is such a spirit still, and yet it is not as it was then. Then each Catholic nation of Europe strove to erect itself into a spiritual independence. But who now dreams of openly attempting such an enterprise? There is contention enough against the Holy See; but men are obliged to mask with plausible words their designs of evil. The age of anti-Popes and subtraction of obedience is over. The central and sole prerogative of sovereignty in the Holy See reigns supreme. It is an age of pontifical acts: for instance, when was there before an act of the Supreme Pontiff so vast or so majestic as that which took the Church of France out of the hands of the first revolution,—recreated, purified, and reconstituted it with a new hierarchy and a new order,—and implanted in it such a renewed principle of vitality that for the last fifty years it has outgrown and overspread the exuberance of all its former history and the abundance of its earlier fruitfulness?

The same power of the Holy See has covered America with new and prolific centres of life and power. It is not fifty years ago when there was but one Bishop in the United States; ten years ago a provincial synod was held in Baltimore of six Archbishops and two-and-twenty suffragans. Again, in Holland, a single act of the Sovereign Pontiff has recalled a hierarchy to life. To come nearer home: after three hundred years' interruption, an episcopate which replaces and continues the hierarchy of St. Gregory the Great, has restored again to England its primitive order, and engrafted us again into the apostolate of the Universal Church.

All these acts were preludes for the manifestation of Catholic unity which has signalised these latter years. There never was a moment when the races of the whole world have so stretched out their hands to the Vicar of Jesus Christ as in the ten or twelve years of the glorious but turbulent Pontificate of Pius IX. The hearts and hands of the faithful throughout the world have been lifted up towards him with an unexampled acclamation of fidelity. I know no more majestic, more royal, more pontifical sight, in the history of the Pontiffs or of the Church, than the Holy Father on the rock of Gaeta issuing, in the moment of his weakness and exile, his three great appeals to the Christian world:—one, the excommunication of the spoilers of the patrimony of the Church; another, a protest to all Christian princes against the wrong that had been done; a third, to all his sons, the episcopate throughout the world. And those three decrees have all wrought their work with power. Supernatural virtue went out with them. The first wrought the downfall of the spoilers who had invaded the Church of God. The second called together the princes of Christendom to do homage to the Vicar of Jesus Christ. The third evoked such a response from the hearts of all the Bishops of the Catholic unity, that in all the annals of the Church there is not to be found anything to compare with the acts of filial love and devotion which the episcopate of the Catholic world laid at his sacred feet.*

It was well said by one of the Bishops of the Church in Ireland the other day, "It is an instinct of nature, that when the head is struck, the hands should lift themselves to guard it." It was but the

---

* See the collection of letters addressed to the Sovereign Pontiff, entitled *L'Orbe Cattolico, a Pio Nono.*

instinct of the mystical body, that, when its head was aimed at, the whole episcopate should surround him in defence. Now perhaps in no former age has the universal consciousness of the body in the sufferings of its head so manifested itself. The age of Cisalpinism, and Gallicanism, and Josephism is past. The unity of life by which the whole body lives in its head, and the universality of the head, by which, as by a real presence everywhere, the Holy See pervades all the provinces of the Catholic unity, has grown to be an instinct and a sense, vivid, powerful, and all-pervading, twice manifested in these last years by acts without any example in the history of the Church,—once in the unanimous voice of the episcopate on the Immaculate Conception,* and again on the temporal sovereignty of the Vicar of Jesus Christ.†

Lastly, the only other point upon which I shall speak is this. We have already seen how the powers and glories of the Holy See have been progressively unfolding; how the time of St. Gregory I. was a period of apostolical missions, converting the nations to the faith; how the time of St. Leo III. was a period

---

* See the response of the Episcopate, in eleven volumes, under the title, *Pareri sulla Definizione dogmatica*, &c.

† See the collection entitled *La Sovranità Temporale*, of which five volumes have already appeared, distributed according to the languages. Nine hundred Bishops have laid their witness and their homage at the feet of Pius IX.

of creating the Christian world; how the time of St. Gregory VII. was a period of purifying the sanctuary of the Church; and how the time of Alexander III. was a period of royalty of government and of ecclesiastical order, when the divine power of the Church directed, by a firm and sacred authority, the civil powers of the world within the sphere of the law of God and of obedience to the faith. Now I observe these powers of the Holy See have been always rising, always culminating. The temporal power in the hands of St. Gregory I. was a fatherly and patriarchal rule over nations not as yet reduced to civil order. In the hands of St. Leo III. it became a power of creating empires. In the hands of St. Gregory VII. it was a scourge to chasten them. In the hands of Alexander III. it was a dynasty, ruling supremely, in the name of God, over the powers of the world. And now in these later times the temporal sovereignty has become a law of the conscience, an axiom of the reason. Through long contests and denials it has passed into the conscience, intellect, and hearts of men. Like the great dogmas of the Church, through controversy it has reached its analysis and expression. It stands by the side of the Immaculate Conception, as a theological certainty, if not a definition. So that I may say there never was a time when the temporal power of the Vicar of the Son of God, though assailed as we see it, was more firmly rooted throughout the whole unity of the Catholic Church in the hearts and convictions of its members; and that by a double process, not only by its own proper evidence, not only by the light of God's dealing with the world, but by contrast. For the nations of Europe have already seen that the society of the world, without the guidance and preservation of the Church of God, resolves itself into confusion. They have seen every form of political society, and the confederations of kingdoms and nations, dissolve and pass away. While all the floating societies of the world have drifted down the stream, the centre of obedience has become more visible. Men have learned from the history of modern Europe that the law which is called the law of nations—that is, the rule of justice which regulates the relations of people with people—has become weak and powerless. And why? Because the nations have broken the bonds which bound them to the centre of obedience, and have shaken off the noble submission to a tribunal higher than man, from which came forth, in other days, the judgments of equity and of justice. It was a dignified obedience to bow to the Vicar of the Son of God, and to remit the arbitration of their griefs to one whom all wills consented to obey. But more than this, in the last seventy years, as we are told by a Catholic writer in France, there have been no less than nine-and-thirty thrones overturned by revolution; two-and-twenty royal families have been driven into exile; five-and-twenty charters or constitutions of civil order have been made, torn up, and trampled upon.* And this because the civil society of the world, which is God's creation, not man's, has been desecrated by revolution. In these latter times they have proudly refused to submit to the guidance and arbitrement of the Church of God, expressed through the Holy See. They have appealed to the revolution, and to the revolution they must go. The civil order of the world is the creation of God. He gives to society by immediate act the sovereignty of power. Society, therefore, is divine. The society of revolution is human, because it springs from the will of man; and that which is created by the will of man may also be torn to pieces by the will of man. What, then, are revolutions, but the will of man tearing to pieces the work of his own hands; or worse, resisting the power "ordained of God"? The Church of God, being a society supernatural and divine, by its constructive and conservative power sustains the order of the world. For God Himself is the Author of both the natural and supernatural orders. He is the Founder of the Society which we call the civil state, as well as of the Church; for He is the God of nature as well as the God of grace. But in these days men claim the political world as their own, and deny all Divine character or sanction to

* La Situation, par Mgr. Gaume, p. 164.

the civil society of nations. They claim its supreme legislation, independently of the Church and of the Divine law, and even against both. And for their external wars and internal conflicts they have no remedy, and no appeal but to numbers and force and military despotisms. They look back with contemptuous compassion upon the ages when the Holy See judged the causes of princes and their peoples, and pronounced upon the contentions of hostile sovereigns. When the Christian grace of justice was in the heart of Europe, and the Christian sentiment of peace and of submission had power over the nations, there was in the Church an influence potent to correct the disquiets of the civil state, and to reduce again to order its casual perturbations. There were no revolutions, as we know them now, in a state subject to the unity and authority of the Church of God. Then, popular discontents were tempered and eliminated by the guidance of a higher principle. But when natural society tears itself away from obedience to the law of God and the unity of the Church, it falls into revolution, and is dissolved by the will of man.

If we need proof, let us look into the Old World and the New. If you desire to see instability in the civil order, look at France, which for sixty years has professed to rest itself upon the revolution of 1789. Look, again, into the New World—into America—where a civil state founded itself within the memory of living men, with all the promise of a great maturity derived from an ancient mother-country. The natural life of one man has outlived its duration. He saw its foundation, and he sees its disruption. The fatal principle of anarchy lay in the beginning; for what the human will creates, the human will may at any time dissolve. The time will surely come, nay, is almost come already, when men will see that the only preservation of the civil order of the world from dissolution is the law of God, and the only record in which the law of God is to be found written is in the Church of God; for the Church of God is the depository of that law, and the unity of the Church is the bond of the unity of kingdoms. They will then return to see that the only authority whereby the Church of God can apply this law is the Holy See. The supreme Pontiff, reigning over the whole Church, legislates and applies the law of God; and therefore, strange as it may seem, the day will come when prince and people, nations and their statesmen, will recognise in the temporal power of the Holy See a divine provision for the maintenance and order of the Christian world, and will return to it as the only solution of the conflicts by which the civil order of the world is broken, the only preservation against the rising flood of revolution. It is so the truth has ever made its way. It has been affirmed and contested; and by contest it has been manifested with more luminous evidence. It has been for a while borne down, and it has risen again, and its resurrection has been with a greater majesty and power. The world has warred upon the temporal power of the Vicar of Jesus Christ. It has shaken the yoke and broken the bonds. In its liberty, it has fallen prostrate; and by its fall its "sense is restored"* to it. From the whole episcopate of the Church has come an universal acclamation of faith in the temporal sovereignty of the Vicar of Jesus Christ as a providential institution upon earth. The consent of the pastors and their flocks witnesses to this deep Catholic instinct, and the voice of the episcopate raises it to a judgment of the Church,† and furnishes the material for a more

* Dan. iv. 33.

† Bellarmine quotes writers of all nations and dignities who have maintained the temporal power of the Pope: twenty-one Italian, sixteen French, twenty Spanish, twelve German, seven English or Scotch. He adds also ten Councils, including two General Councils, Lateran four, and Lyons two, in which the temporal power was recognised; and sums up in these words: "Si hæc non est Ecclesiæ Catholicæ vox, ubi obsecro eam inveniemus?" *De Potestate Papæ, contra Barclaium*, inter Opuscula, pp. 831-845.

The Theological Faculty of the University of Cagliari has given the following answers to the propositions of the Sardinian Ministry:—

"Prop. 1. That the temporal power of the Pope is a fact in its very nature accidental and of human origin.

Answer: Although the temporal power of the Sovereign Pontiff may not be immediately a Divine institution, nevertheless, it is clearly a fact of a most special Providence.

Prop. 2. That the temporal power of the Pope may therefore

solemn utterance. The very conflict which seemed to threaten it has defined and published it with a greater light. And the nations of Europe, returning to themselves from the excesses of instability, and wearied with the terrors of revolution, are beginning to recognise the fountain of their own former peace and greatness. Paradox as it may seem, this may be said to be the period of the temporal sovereignty, both of its trials and of its manifestation.

Now in these many characters the present glories of the Holy See surpass its former days, and give promise of a hereafter into which I will not venture.

The mutation of races and kingdoms is the per-

be lessened, and even extinguished, with no injury to his spiritual power and religious liberty.

Answer: History clearly shows that the Sovereign Pontiff was always either a temporal sovereign (in fact, or in right), or else oppressed by persecution, and in an habitual state of martyrdom.

Prop. 3. That in the natural order of things the temporal power of the Pope is destitute of every principle of perpetuity; and instead of being useful, is injurious both to the Church and to the State.

Answer: The Sovereign Pontiff Pope Pius IX. has more than once expressly declared that, in the present condition of society, the temporal power of the Holy See is both most useful, and even necessary for the liberty of the Church, and the independence and sovereignty of the acts of her visible Head. This pontifical declaration has been accepted with unparalleled unanimity by the whole Catholic Episcopate, from which the Spirit of Truth, the perpetual life of the body of the Church, never departs.

Prop. 4. That it is moreover necessary for the Holy Father

petual running contrast to the immutability of the Holy See. It has renewed its relations again and again with hordes and races, monarchies and republics, empires and confederations. It is no new thing for the Vicar of Jesus Christ to create and to inaugurate, to recognise and to renew, another form of Christian society, or a new combination of ancient Europe. What has been, may be. We have an undying and an unbounded faith in the Church of God. We have received "an immovable kingdom." The changes around it pass like winds of the wilderness. It outlives empires, as it outlives men. It is never

not to refuse to treat with the Italian Government, in order to secure, by that means, greater facility and more independence in the exercise of his Catholic powers.

Answer: The answer to this proposition clearly flows from the answers already given."

Since the foregoing note was written, the address of the Episcopate assembled in Rome in the Consistory of Whit-Monday last, has added a splendid and final enunciation of this subject matter; of which it is enough to quote the following passage:

"We recognise the temporal sovereignty of the Holy See as a necessary thing, and manifestly instituted by the providence of God. Nor do we hesitate to declare, in the present condition of human things, that this temporal sovereignty is absolutely required for the good and free government of the Church and of men's souls. It was clearly necessary that the Roman Pontiff, the Head of the whole Church, should not be the subject of any sovereign, nay, nor the guest of any; but that, established in his own dominions and kingdom, he should be his own master; and in noble, peaceful, and gentle liberty, should defend and protect the Catholic Faith, and rule and govern the whole Christian commonwealth."

old or young, but "yesterday, and to-day, and the same for ever."*

Hitherto we have been tracing its path in the historical order, and this history of the Church is like the history of Jesus in the Gospels. It is full of sorrow, suffering, and passion. But we see there the life of the Son of God, accomplishing His work and establishing His kingdom. We have seen, too, the narrative of the Vicars of Jesus Christ written on the page of the world's history, and, like that of their Divine Master, it has been a history of suffering, of passion, and of conflict; but so they too have been doing their work, and establishing His kingdom upon earth. "We have an immovable kingdom." Kingdoms which sprung from the will of man have been and are not; but the Church of God cannot be moved. Eighteen hundred years of conflict have thrown out into relief and light its divine stability, its imperishable life, its indivisible unity, its infallible voice, its perpetual visibility, its temporal sovereignty, its twofold prerogatives, spiritual and temporal, whereby it has ruled the destinies of the world, and will reign, even through conflict, to the end. Come what may, the Church of God, both centre and circumference, is immovable. The persecutions of a heathen world could not shake it; the persecutions of Antichrist will be broken upon it. "Whosoever shall fall on

* Heb. xiii. 8.

this stone shall be broken; but on whomsoever it shall fall, it shall grind him to powder."* The storm which sweeps over the mountain clings to it for a moment, and seems to overpower it, but in an instant it is rent asunder and hurried away. The persecutions of Antichrist will be but as the storm upon the mountain. The Church has already once worshipped and offered the unbloody sacrifice in Catacombs, in deserts, and in hiding-places, and that for generations. Yet all the world beheld the "city seated on a hill, which cannot be hid." Its very martyrdoms made it visible. Its Pontiffs reigned in Rome, all pagan as it was; they have reigned over the City of the Seven Hills in all the alternations of its destinies,—in its splendour and its desolation, in its sieges and its deliverances,—Bishops of Rome, Successors of St. Peter, and Vicars of Jesus Christ. And as it has been said, so it shall be, in all and through all, unto the consummation of the world.† Even now, in the dimness of

---

* St. Matt. xxi. 44.

† "Ob temporum calamitates coguntur interdum Pontifices abesse, aut certe principum potentiâ coacti: ut forte accidit quo tempore Romana curia erat in Gallia. Quod dicitur de urbis vastatione, credibile est Deum nunquam permissurum ut portæ inferi contra eam prævaleant ob sanctorum Petri et Pauli successionem, sedis Apostolicæ dignitatem ac Ecclesiæ totius utilitatem, et ita intelligimus sæpe fuisse præteritis temporibus divinitus servatam; præcipue tempore Leonis Papæ, ut habet historia vulgata. Unde Chrysostomus 2 ad Thessal. docet regnum Romanorum duraturum usque ad Antichristum, eumque contra Romanum Pontificem potentissime

the present, we see the outlines and the preludes of a higher and more glorious manifestation of the kingdom of God on earth. They who will hereafter look back upon the age of Pius IX. will see in its breadth and maturity that which we see only in its germ; and the faint lights which streak our sky, and even the clouds which darken it, will be to them more luminous and splendid than the ages of the Leos and the Gregories are to us. To them it is reserved to see the ingathering of the fields which even now are whitening to the harvest in the virgin soil of the East and West, and the second spring which even now is rising in its sap and blade, under the decay of the old Christian society of Europe. Ours is but the seed-time of the charity and industry and world-wide unity of the mystical Body in its love and loyalty to the twofold Sovereignty of the Vicar of Christ. "Euntes ibant et flebant mittentes semina sua." It is ours to sow in tears; they who come after shall reap in joy; and the retrospect of their days will outshine the retrospect of ours. "The land that was desolate and impassable shall be glad, and the wilderness shall rejoice, and shall flourish like the lily. It shall bud forth and blossom, and shall rejoice with joy and praise; the glory of Libanus is given to it: the beauty of Carmel and Saron; and

pugnaturum." Suarez, *de Fide Disp.* x., de Summo Pontifice, sect. iii. 11.

they shall see the glory of the Lord, and the beauty of our God."* "For Sion's sake I will not hold my peace, and for the sake of Jerusalem I will not rest, till her Just One come forth in brightness, and her Saviour be lighted as a lamp. And the Gentiles shall see thy Just One, and all the kings thy glorious One; and thou shalt be called by a new name, which the mouth of the Lord shall name, and thou shalt be a crown of glory in the hand of the Lord; and a royal diadem in the hand of thy God."†

Then, as St. Paul says, "We have grace;" our confidence is not in the help of man, but in the grace of God. It is not only the facts of the past that give us grounds and reasons of fearless trust; our confidence is in grace, that is, in supernatural power. We confide not in the intervention of human agents, but in the hand of God. And for this we have three sure pledges. First, the promises of God. The Son of God has said, "The gates of hell shall not prevail against the Church." He does not say they shall not prevail against the spiritual power of the Church. He makes no distinction or reserves. He says they shall not prevail against the Church, that is, in all the fulness of its complex majesty and the array of its prerogatives of power. Again, the Holy Ghost says, "We have an immovable kingdom." If none can move it, certainly none can dissolve a particle of

* Isaias xxxv. 1, 2.   † Ibid. lxii. 1-3.

its Divine order. Next, we have the love of God for the society of men. In the ancient Greek liturgy, God is called upon as the "Lover of men." He loves them not only in the order of grace, but in the order of nature. God loves households and families, homes and nations, and races and peoples; and the civil society of mankind, even though it be not in the order of grace, is an object of His compassion: for it is the power which maintains the order, and promotes the welfare and civilisation of mankind. God does not will to abandon human society, though men with evil principles and without God in the world may labour to heave it from the foundations in which He has built it in grace. Though the world forsake God, He will not abandon the world till its judgment is full. He loves to watch over it. His providence is always benign. Not a sparrow falls to the ground without our Father. How much less, then, will He suffer the peace and order of the nations of the world to be shattered, in which millions of innocent would suffer with the guilty.* Thirdly, and above all, God loves His Church, for it is the mystical body of His Son. And the love He has for His Son passes to His mystical body. He loves the Church in His Son. As St. Paul says, "He hath graced us in His beloved Son."† The Church, too, is

---

* "Sanabiles fecit nationes orbis terrarum, et non est in illis medicamentum exterminii." Lib. Sap. i. 14.   † Eph. i. 6.

His Spouse; and He loves the Church as the bridegroom loves the bride. And the Church is the Mother of the elect, the instrument of his predestination, and the manifestation of Himself. Therefore God loves the Vicar of His incarnate Son. He loves with an eminent and special love him who is the representative of His Son on earth, who bears the character and marks of Jesus above all other men. With a singular and personal love He loves him for his office as the Vicar of His Son. But He loves him, too, because he is most like Him, not only in office, but in suffering. The Sovereign Pontiff bears the cross; and bears the cross for us. On him is laid the sorrows of the whole Church on earth; to him is given to suffer in its behalf. His is a life of martyrdom, because he is the witness and the image of the Son of God on Calvary. And God loves him too for his own sake, because he is the fulfilment of the promise, "He that hath My words and keepeth them, he it is that loveth Me; and he that loveth Me shall be loved of My Father, and I will love him." * Such is the manifold love of God which encircles at this hour the person of our beloved Pontiff and Father. For in all the line of those who have reigned over the Church, there is none in whom the faith and law of Jesus, and the graces of justice and mercy, clemency and generosity, long-suffering and patience,

* St. John xiv. 21.

calmness and confidence in God, have shone more bright and luminous. Through all these long years of wrong there is one whose faith has never wavered, whose hope has never been shaken, and whose charity has never been chilled. He has stood as the pillar of light, when all around were dark. Against him no man has spoken and has passed uncondemned. No weapon forged against him shall prosper, though for a time evil may seem to have its full success. In a little while all the power of men shall consume away, and the place thereof shall know it no more.

As I said in the beginning, the human will is striving, and the multitudinous wills of men, like the tossing of a great sea, are lifting themselves against him; but the Lord sitteth above the waterfloods. He will encompass the Church on every side, and His presence is as a wall of fire round the Vicar of His Son. With such a sure unfailing trust, "let us serve" "with fear," and fearing God, fear nothing else. Nothing can harm the Church of God, nothing can harm the Vicar of Jesus Christ. For through His Church God is with us; and in the person of Pius IX., Jesus reigns on earth, and "He must reign until He hath put all enemies under His feet."*

---

* 1 Cor. xv. 25.

INDEX.

ABOLITION of law of marriage, 73, 74.
Abomination of desolation, 158.
Acknowledgment of a form of faith as binding on the conscience, 72.
"Adscripti glebæ," lviii.
Alexander III., picture of the times of, 208; epoch of period of supremacy over the powers of the world, 208.
Ambrose, St., xxv.
Antichrist, characteristics of, 103, 119; hindrance to manifestation of, 117; the principle of the French Revolution, 131; principles of in the ascendant, 134; Mahomet a type of, 159.
Apostles, twofold jurisdiction given to, 7.
Apotheosis of human pride, what, 100.
Aristotle, xlii.
Attacks on the patrimony of the Church, 55.
"Auctorem Fidei," the Bull, xxxix.
Authorities, two ultimate, 84.
Avignon, schism of, 91.
Avitus, St., xxv.

BARBARISM, a consequence of the dissolution of the Temporal Power, 34, 56.
Belisarius, Britain in the time of, 67.
Bellarmine, xxxv.
Bishops, response of nine hundred, 230 *note;* consistory of on Whit-Monday 1862, 238.
Bishops of Rome, for 1200 years temporal princes, 16; the first seed of Christian Europe, 16.
Body, sacramental and natural, of our Lord, 7; mystical of our Lord, 7.
Branches of the Temporal Sovereignty, two, 5.
Breakspear, Nicolas (Adrian IV.), 50.
Bull, "Auctorem Fidei," xxxix.

CAGLIARI, the opinion of its University on the Temporal Power, 236.
Catholic Church, *vide* Church.
Catholic view of Holy Sacraments, viii.; civilisation, 132; traditions of limitation of civil power, 61.
Cardinal Ferretti, saying of, lxviii.
Causes of the Revolution in the States of the Church, 68.
Cerularius, xxxiv.
Charlemagne, declared a Roman patrician, 41; restitution of, 15.
Charles, St., charity of, 20.
China of Christendom, what, 47.
Christendom, created by the Church, 185; civil order of, 35; productive cause and root of, 37; dissolution of, 76.
Christian Europe, a new creation, 39; society growing weaker, 133; doomed, 134; centre of, 143; civilisation created by the Popes, 127; colonies, 21.
Christianity, formal antagonist of, 89; the only "societas illicita," 151; the one exception to toleration, 152.
Church, twofold mission of, 36; an unlawful society for 300 years, 9; possessed of highest rights, 18; necessary to liberty, 135; belief in a visible, 3; a supernatural society, 128; spiritual and supernatural sovereignty vested in, 5; creator of Christendom, 185; future resurrection and ascension of, 148; Jesus Himself, 177; cannot be endangered, 177; the sole sustaining power of Christendom, 185; a kingdom, 155; never recedes, 184; binding on the will, 155; guide of families and households, 181; guide of nations and peoples, 181; refusal of toleration to, 156; the sole tribunal of conscience, 182; four notes of, xxiii.; three properties of, xxiii.; three endowments of, xxiii.; an object of sense, of reason, and of faith, xxiii.; reduction of to a school of religious philosophy, lxv.; reduction of to an association for charitable works, lxv.; sole principle of stability, 191; unchangingness of, 192; indissoluble constitution of, 218; industry of legislation of, 223; patrimonies of, 20; civil mission of, 27, 35, 127.
Civil law, property not created by, 19.
Civil mission of the Church, Temporal Power necessary to, 27, 35.
Civil powers, desecration of, 162.
Civil and spiritual powers, conflict between, 186-188.
Civilisation, Christian, created by the Popes, 127; in revolt from the Christian Church, lvi.; Catholic conquered, by natural, 132; of nineteenth century, boastful, lxi.

Clement VII., picture of times of, 210; epoch of a period of resplendence, 215.
Comte, errors of, 95-100.
Confliction of civil and spiritual powers, 209.
Conscience, tribunal of, 182.
Constantine, donation of, 12.
Council, spiritual and civil powers in, 43; of Nice, xx.; of Florence, xx.; of Orange, xx.; Trent, xx.
Courage, Christian, characteristics of, 170.
Creator and maker of property, God, 19.

DATE of independence of Italy and Rome, 14.
Deification of humanity, consequence of Protestantism, 92.
Democracy, tendency of government to, 133; exhaustion of powers of government, 133; instability of, 235; foretold by St. Hippolytus, 74.
Deposing power of the Pope, nature of, 46.
Desecrated power, what, 72.
Desecration of civil powers, 162.
Desideratum among Englishmen, what, 4.
Desiderius, King of the Lombards, xlviii.
Despotisms, where especially found, 60; effect of dissolution of the Temporal Power, 60; prevalence of, 135.
De Maistre, Count, li.
De Tocqueville, 133.
Dissolution of the Temporal Power, effects of, 56-60.
Distinctions, national, abolished, 28; the true, between spiritual and temporal, 5.
Dogma of faith, conditions of, xxxviii.
Dominion, civil, Rome, excluded from, 16.
Donation of Constantine, 12.
Donoso Cortez, 134.

ECCLESIASTICAL polity, axioms of, abolished by Reformation, xx.
Elective monarchy, Roman State the only example of, 50.
Emancipation by the Church, 22; of slaves by St. Gregory, 22.
Emperor, the Roman, 9, 209; the heathen, motive of Christian obedience to, 11.
England, by what organised, 43; sovereignty of received by the indirect providence of God, 24; no nation so easily deceived, 65;

Protestant, the least intellectual of Protestant countries, 90 ; material prosperity of, 163; errors of, material and rationalistic, xxi. ; its traditional animosity against the Holy See, xx.

Error, progression in manifestation of, xx.

Eternal and temporal truly opposed, 5.

Europe, Christian, the first seed of, 16 ; a new creation, 39 ; special and personal action of Pontiffs on, 44 ; principle of obedience in, 45 ; created by priestly government, 52.

Eusebius, xxxiii.

Faith, conditions of dogma of, xxxviii. ; divine, substitution of human opinion for, 85 ; light of, interpreter of history, 102.

Ferretti, Cardinal, saying of, lxviii.

First principles, the lack of, among Englishmen, 3.

Free exercise of spiritual power, 135.

French Revolution, paganism unchained, 75.

Fulfilment of the civil mission of the Church, 3.

Gallican liberties, 91.

Germany, pantheism of, 92.

Ghost, Holy, denial of, 85.

Gnosticism of our days, vi., 90.

God, the knowledge of, springing from the Holy See, 45 ; the true creator and maker of property, 19.

Government of priests created modern Europe, 52.

Greek schism, the China of Christendom, 47.

Greek schismatics, law of marriage abolished by, 74.

Gregory I. the Great, St., 22 ; picture of times of, 199, xxxvi. ; his time, epoch of conversion of nations, 215.

Gregory II., xlii.

Gregory VII., St., 1. ; letter of, 204.

HERESY existing in every age, 87 ; reappearance of, 88 ; smitten with its death-blow, 224.

Hippolytus, St., prophecy of, 74 ; words of, 134.

History, knowledge of, a desideratum, 2 ; of Christian Europe, what, 55 ; only truly read in the light of faith, 102.

Holy Ghost, denial of, 85.

Holy See, limitations imposed by, 46.

Hostility against the Supreme Pontiff, 6.

Huss, xxxiv.

IGNORANCE, consequence of Protestantism, 225.
Immaculate Conception, 226.
Immutability of the Holy See, 238.
Incarnation, belief in, a primary postulate, 3; denial of, 86, 161; nationalism abolished by, 91; the foundation of the political order of Europe hitherto, 129.
Increase, law of, 218.
Independence of Italy and Rome, date of 14.
Indifference, consequence of Protestantism, 225.
Infidelity, consequence of Protestantism, 225.
Intellect, indistinctness of, 31.
Irenæus, St., xxxiii.

JEROME, St., interpretation of, 84.
Jews, people of, interpenetrating all nations, 146; deadly antagonists to the Christian Church, 145.

KEYSTONE of Christendom, 47.
Knowledge of God springing from the Holy See, 45; of history, a desideratum, 2.

LAING's Notes on Europe, 60.
Latter days, first glory of, 220; second glory of, 222.
Law of marriage abolished, 73.
Legislation of Church, industry of, 223.
Leo the Isaurian, xlvii.
Leo. St., picture of times of, 201; epoch of creation of Christian Europe, 215.
Letters of St. Gregory, 204; of Pope Stephen II., 41.
Liberals, illiberality of, 156.
Liberty, the Church necessary to, 135.
Lombardy, the war in, 70.
Luther, xxi., xxxiv.

MACCHIAVELLI, xxxvi.
Mahomet, type of Antichrist, 159.
Maistre, Count de, li.
Marriage, dissolved by Greek schism, Protestantism, and French Revolution, 73.
Martin I., St., xlii.
Martyrs, thirty, among the Roman Pontiffs, 185.
Matthew, St., prophecy of, 144.

Monarchy, made a free institution by the Holy See, 45; elective, Roman States example of, 50; mitigated by Catholic tradition, 61.
Morell, History of Modern Philosophy, 92-94.
Motives of Christian obedience, 11.
Mysteries of godliness and impiety, 105.

NAPOLEON I., saying of, 77.
Nationalism, in religion schism, in politics revolution, 28; consequence of Protestantism, 90; seen in Reformation, 91; abolished by the Incarnation, 91.

OBEDIENCE, Christian, motive of, 11; preserved Europe, 45; taught by the Holy See, 46.

PAGANISM unchained, French Revolution, 75; restoration of, 113.
Pantheism, deification of humanity, 92; boundless egotism, 100.
Paschal controversy, xxxiii.
Passion, sign of our Lord's presence, 178; of Jesus Christ shared by His Church, 197.
Patrician of Rome, xlviii.; highest civil dignity, 41.
Patrimonies of the Holy See, twenty-three in number, 20, 199.
Pelagius and Pelagianism, xx., xxi.
Pepin, King, xlvii., 14.
Persecution, five signs of one approaching, 148, 163; of truth, 151; present, in Italy, 157.
Pius IX., allocution of, 166; three appeals of, 229; character of 170; opposed by the world, lxiii.; fortitude of, 193, lxiii.
Politics, divorced from Revelation, 81.
Popes, sovereigns among sovereigns, lxiii.; guardians of Christian faith, lxiii.; sprung from humble life, 51; peaceful, 52; "Pontifices almificos," liv.; possess exclusive right to Rome, 183; prerogatives of, 142; dethronement of, 161; subject to none, 181; reigned for 1200 years, 16; centre of Christian society, 143; first example of Christian monarchy, 16; creators of Christian civilisation, 127; Vicars of Jesus Christ, 142; thirty martyred, 185; thirty banished, 188; four imprisoned, four unable to set foot in Rome, seven reigned at Avignon, nine driven out of Rome, 185-189.
Positivism of Comte, 92; sacred formula of, 99.

INDEX. 253

Power, Temporal, of the Holy See, in what sense a Divine institution, xxx.; supernatural character of, xxvii.; not a material object of a dogma of faith, xxxviii.; not absolutely necessary to spiritual power, 26; but for its free and peaceful exercise, 27; shelter of the spiritual, 25; two branches of, 5; distinct elements of, 179; united to the spiritual, xxviii., xxix., 219; difficulties in its treatment, xix. ; cumulus of evidence in its regard, xxviii. ; recognised by ten councils, two of which were general, xxxvi. ; recognised by the "magisterium juge Ecclesiæ," xxxvii. ; by the voice of the Episcopate, 230, 238 *note ;* writers and opinions on, 236 *note ;* a theological certainty and law of conscience, 231; necessary to the civil mission of the Church, 27, 35; protest against nationalism, 28; six different periods of, patience and martyrdom, xl.; liberation, xli.; interregnum, xliv. ; paternal dictatorship, xliv. ; popular election, xlvi. ; unbroken possession for more than 1000 years, l. ; opposition of the world to, lxiii. ; not to be dissolved by popular will, liii.; usurped, 55; assailed, 190; restored, 190; effects of its dissolution, 34, 56; keystone of Christianity, 47; finally liberated, xix.

Power of the Church, depression of, 135.

Powers, sacerdotal and royal, two conservative principles, 46.

Principles, first, lack of, 3.

Property not the creation of civil law, 19.

Prosperity, temporal, not a test of God's favour, 178.

Protestantism, despotism of, 60; formal antagonist of Christianity, 89; revolt against the supernatural, xxi. ; against sacramental grace, xxi. ; with Pelagianism, the two extremes of heresy, xx. ; modern, xxi. ; dark future of, 89; reproductiveness of, 90; of England, pabulum for every error, 90; Gnosticism of our day, 90; consequences of, 90, 225; its false interpretations of Holy Scripture, 165; no longer a religion, but a political system, 225.

Pudentiana, St., 18.

Pulcheria, Empress, xlvi.

RATIONALISM, consequence of Protestantism, 225.

Reformation, Anglican, 91; impotence of, 155; abolished first axioms of ecclesiastical polity, xx.

Regalia Petri, xxxvi.

Revelation, generally excluded from politics, 81, 129.

Revolt, definition of, 83; three characters of, 85.

Revolution, in the States of the Church, five causes of, 68; French, 75; outbreak of antichristian spirit, 131; of 1789, 1830, and 1848, identical in principle, 131; consequences of, 232, 233; involves the guilt of rebellion, lx.

Roccaberti, Bibliotheca Pontificia, xxiii.

Rome, ancient, type of the Church, "Roma nunquam recedit," 183.

Rome, City of, seven times sacked, once wholly destroyed, 189; nine times in the hands of usurpers, 190; saved only by the Roman Pontiffs, 14; excluded from civil dominion, 16; purgation by fire and blood, 14, 165; patrician of, 41.

Rome, See of, centre of the Church, 37; leader, guide, and legislator, 44; personal action of, 44; guardian of the knowledge of God, 45; its immutability, 236; hindrance to the manifestation of Antichrist, 127; teaches obedience and clemency, 46; its deposing power, 46; its imperishable vitality and invincible endurance, 179; sovereignty of, 180; key and centre of all supernatural action, xxv.

SACRIFICE, Christian, taking away of, 157.

Sacraments, not to be treated by natural calculus, xxii.

Sardinia, inchoate schism of, lvii.

Schism, spirit of, in Piedmont and Portugal, lvii.; Greek, the China of Christendom, 47.

Scripture, falsely interpreted by Protestant writers, 165.

Sects, cannot bind the will, 155.

Signs, five, of a coming persecution, 148.

Slavery, gradually abolished by the Church, 22.

Society, twofold, natural and supernatural, 128; natural, re-establishment of, 162; civil, a divine institution, 233, 243.

Sovereignty, inherent in the person of the Supreme Pontiff, 179, 181; local and temporal, 179, 182; purchased by thirty martyrdoms, 185; its definition, 180; of the Church, work of God, 197.

Spain, civilisation of, owing to the Church, 43.

Stability, sole principle of, 191.

Stapleton, xxxv.

Stephen II., letter of, 41.

Suarez, xxxv., 180, 240.

Sufferings of the Popes, 186-188.

Supernatural element in the world, 114.

"Tædium de Deo," shown in rebellion against the Supreme Pontiff, lvi.
Tertullian, 9, xxxiii.
Theology, its periods of conception, definition, and scientific manifestation, xxxv.
Times, present, difficult to appreciate, 198.
Tocqueville (De), quoted, 133.
Toledo, eighteen councils of, created the civilisation of Spain, 43.
Toleration, one exception to, 152; denied to the Church by liberals, 156.
Truth, indifference to, 148; contempt and persecution of, 150, 151; testimony to, 173.

War, offensive, never waged by the Popes, 52.
Will, not bound by Protestant sects, 155.
World, modern, its agents, 146; its hostility to the Incarnation, 161.

THE END.

PRINTED BY BALLANTYNE, HANSON AND CO.
EDINBURGH AND LONDON

www.ingramcontent.com/pod-product-compliance
Lightning Source LLC
Chambersburg PA
CBHW030739230426
43667CB00007B/770